Back to *Basics*

Cabinet
Construction

Back to *Basics*

Cabinet Construction

*Straight Talk for Today's **Woodworker***

By the Editors at Skills Institute Press

skills institute press

Distributed By
Fox Chapel Publishing

FOX CHAPEL
PUBLISHING

© 2011 by Skills Institute Press LLC
"Back to Basics" series trademark of Skills Institute Press
Published and distributed in North America by Fox Chapel Publishing Company, Inc., East Petersburg, PA.

Cabinet Construction is an original work, first published in 2011.

Portions of text and art previously published by and reproduced under license with Direct Holdings Americas Inc.

ISBN 978-1-56523-529-8

Library of Congress Cataloging-in-Publication Data

Cabinet construction.
    p. cm. -- (Back to basics)
Includes index.
ISBN 978-1-56523-529-8
1. Cabinetwork--Amateurs' manuals. I. Fox Chapel Publishing.
TT197.C2125 2011
684.1'6--dc22
                        2010037795

To learn more about the other great books from Fox Chapel Publishing,
or to find a retailer near you, call toll-free 800-457-9112 or visit us at
www.FoxChapelPublishing.com.

Note to Authors: We are always looking for talented authors to write new books
in our area of woodworking, design, and related crafts. Please send a brief letter
describing your idea to Acquisition Editor, 1970 Broad Street, East Petersburg, PA 17520.

Printed in China
First printing: July 2011

Contents

What You Can Learn

Carcase Construction, page 18

The basic box—or carcase—featured in this chapter has long been the starting point of many types of furniture, but there are seemingly limitless variations on a basic design.

Frame-and-Panel Construction, page 46

Frame-and-panel offers a solution to wood's tendency to warp, shrink, and expand in response to temperature and humidity.

Drawers, page 74

A drawer's most basic function is to hold things, but it must also slip in and out of the piece of furniture without jamming or chattering.

Doors, page 102

Assembling a door demands the same care as building the piece it accompanies.

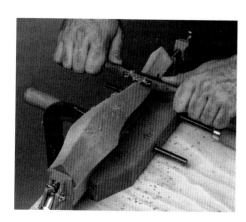

Legs, page 122

The legs must support the rest of the furniture, but they also play an equally important aesthetic role.

Shaker Chest

I remember when I first came under the spell of Shaker furniture. Wandering the halls of the Shaker Museum in Old Chatham, New York, I was transported to another time, awestruck at the feeling evoked by those simple pieces. The Shakers were a religious, Utopian society that flourished in New England and the Midwest in the 19th Century. Their furniture designs were born at least partially out of a desire to lead a simpler, more religious existence. In their quest, they achieved a purity of design rivaled only by the work created for the Buddhist temples of Japan.

For lack of a more descriptive term, I have dubbed the cupboard and case of drawers shown here "The Utility Chest." Its prototype, whose original purpose is no longer known, was built in Enfield, Connecticut, around 1825–1850. The surprising off-center placement of the two small drawers demonstrates Shaker design at its height, pointing not only to a purity of form, but to the asymmetry of human existence as well. The original function of those two drawers may be lost today, but it is sure to have been a practical one.

The utility chest is built of pine and measures 17 inches deep, 31 inches wide and 71 inches high. Its construction is relatively simple and can be accomplished using a combination of standard casework-, door-, and drawer-making techniques. For a project like this, however, attention should be paid to the layout of the design. I find it helpful to do a full-scale drawing on either a large piece of cardboard or the freshly sanded top of my workbench to ensure that the scale is correct.

Finishing this piece was a considerable challenge. Most cabinetmakers are not finishers. It should be pointed out that the trick to any good finish is to build it up gradually with multiple thin coats. In this case, a light yellow paint was used first, then steel wool, followed by a wash of pumpkin paint, more steel wool, and an application of orange shellac to warm up the yellow. The finishing touch comes with a light coating of varnish or lacquer to protect the shellac.

- Ian Ingersoll

Ian Ingersoll owns a cabinet construction shop in West Cornwall, Connecticut, specializing in Shaker furniture.

Craftsmanship

The inspiration for this cabinet came from a small billet of Swiss pear given to me seven years ago. I felt that it had taken me at least that long to acquire the skills to work with this beautiful, but somewhat difficult wood. The pear was a dark golden pink and had a soft appearance. I designed the cabinet to highlight the wood's wonderful surface and its ability to stand up to the shaping of delicate edge profiles. I wanted to show off the raw material.

I resawed the pear into veneers, a scant ⅛-inch thick, bookmatched them, and glued them to a plywood core. I then edge banded and shaped the top and bottom. I doweled the sides to small 1¼-inch posts, needing solid wood for the joints with the legs. Next, I doweled the top, bottom and sides together precisely, using one dowel per inch. I finished all the pieces before gluing up. The legs, made from jarrah, were then notched, glued and screwed to the corners of the cabinet.

Pear is as demanding as it is beautiful. The joinery must be tight and perfect; slight imperfections are very noticeable. I spent a great deal of time sharpening my planes to get the edge joints crisp and the surfaces unflawed. The jarrah, on the other hand, was a pleasure to work with. It planed in any direction, sawed and shaped easily, and took the light oil finish I applied very well. I finished the pear with several thin coats of blond shellac, bringing out its color and surface markings.

Inside the cabinet are two drawers, each made of Andaman padauk and camphor. Under the drawers, in the middle of the interior, is a curved shelf. I made the L-shaped knife hinges and door pulls from patinated brass.

My inspiration comes from several sources, including my teacher Jim Krenov, Greek architecture, Japanese craft and French cabinetmaker Emile Ruhlmann. What is important in everything I make is that the influences are balanced, the craftsmanship is the best I can achieve, and the results pleasing.

- Michael Burns

Michael Burns teaches cabinet construction at College of the Redwoods in Fort Bragg, California.

Writing Desk

Being self-taught, I rely on a very informal approach to design. My furniture tends to evolve as I proceed through the construction process. For example, seeking an alternative to the common tapered leg, and inspired by 1920s cabinetmakers Jules Leleu and Emile Ruhlmann, I developed a multifaceted fluted leg. To do this, I designed a fixture for my spindle shaper that allowed me to profile and flute the twelve facets of the leg. After much trial and error, I had one prototype leg and a whole new challenge: Namely, how to attach the leg to a table or desk apron. Eventually, I made a mock-up of a desk with a diagonal corner post and attached the leg to the post. Presenting the leg at a 45° angle produced visually pleasing details that became the inspiration for this lady's writing desk.

To construct the desk, I used a combination of mortise-and-tenon and dovetail joinery. The drawers are also dovetailed. I chose Bubinga—African Rosewood—which is remarkable for its striking figure and color. The grain pattern in the desk top was achieved by resawing a plank into $\frac{1}{10}$-inch-thick veneer. A wonderful streak of light-colored sapwood graces one edge of the plank. When the sapwood edges were glued together into bookmatched (mirror image) panels, the results were spectacular. Around the perimeter of the top and where the surrounding frame meets the panels, I inlaid a thin line of curly maple to add visual texture and to emphasize the frame-and-panel effect. Adding curly maple pulls and a cockbead around the drawers further enhanced the color contrast. All these features work together to evoke a sense of functional elegance.

While this desk is obviously a complex piece, you should not feel intimidated; every craftsman was once a novice. You can, with the right instructional information, along with patience and practice, master all of the techniques that you will need. Remember, though, the museums can wait to enshrine your masterpiece, so don't bite off more than you can chew right away. Start with simple projects that allow you to practice your skills and develop your design sense. A simple project well executed is far better than an elaborate piece that has been shoddily made. There will be failures and mistakes along the way, but this, too, is part of the process of learning. The main objective is to enjoy your work and do the best you can.

-Terry Moore

Originally from Wales, Terry Moore designs and builds fine furniture in Newport, New Hampshire.

Cabinet Construction

The first step in any Cabinet Construction project is to select and prepare your stock. As shown below, not all the wood at a lumberyard is free of defects, so it is important to choose boards carefully.

Whether you are building an armoire or a toy box, most stock is readied in roughly the same way. The procedures illustrated on pages 15 to 17 cover the basic techniques. For rough, or unsurfaced lumber, first pass one face across the jointer, then one edge, producing two surfaces that are at 90° to each other. Next, plane the second face, making it parallel to the first. Now you are ready to rip your stock to width and crosscut it to length. For dressed, or surfaced lumber, you only have to joint one edge, then rip and crosscut. Before gluing up a piece of furniture be sure to sand any surfaces that will be difficult to reach afterwards.

Choosing Lumber

Common wood defects

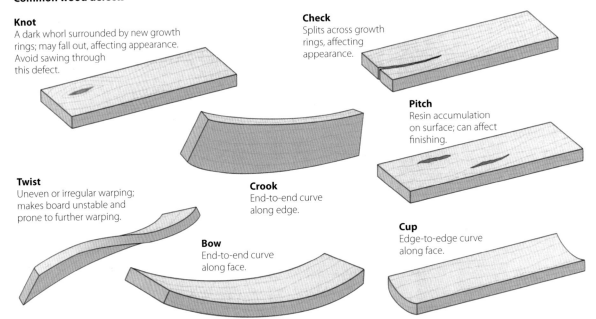

Knot
A dark whorl surrounded by new growth rings; may fall out, affecting appearance. Avoid sawing through this defect.

Check
Splits across growth rings, affecting appearance.

Pitch
Resin accumulation on surface; can affect finishing.

Twist
Uneven or irregular warping; makes board unstable and prone to further warping.

Crook
End-to-end curve along edge.

Cup
Edge-to-edge curve along face.

Bow
End-to-end curve along face.

Selecting stock for cabinet construction

Wood is available in two broad categories: hardwood and softwood. Although the terms are botanical rather than descriptive, hardwoods, such as mahogany and cherry, are preferable for most cabinet construction projects because they are, in fact, generally harder. Before buying lumber, examine it carefully. Check its color, texture and grain patterns, and select stock that you find visually appealing. Lumber is usually milled in one of two ways: Quarter-sawed, or edge-grained, lumber has a tough surface and is generally stable; plain-sawed, or flat-grained lumber, although less expensive, is more prone to warping and shrinking. Whatever type of wood you buy, choose kiln-dried lumber, and watch out for defects. Some of those shown above only affect appearance, but others can make the wood difficult to cut, joint or plane. You can avoid defects by buying "select" lumber when possible.

Jointing a Board

Maintaining proper pressure on the outfeed table

For most operations, set a cutting depth between ⅛ and 1⁄16 inch. To joint a board edge, feed the stock slowly into the cutterhead, pressing its face against the fence while keeping the edge flat on the jointer tables. Be sure to feed the workpiece so the knives are cutting with the grain. Continue feeding the stock until your right hand approaches the outfeed table. Then reverse the position of your hands without stopping the cut. Gradually slide your left hand toward the back of the workpiece, maintaining pressure against the fence *(right)*. Shift your right hand farther back on the stock to maintain downward pressure just to the outfeed side of the knives. Continue these handover-hand movements until the pass is completed. To joint the face of a board, follow the same procedures, using push blocks to feed the stock.

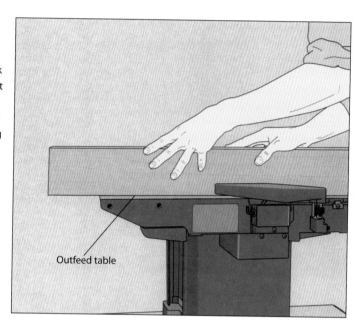

Outfeed table

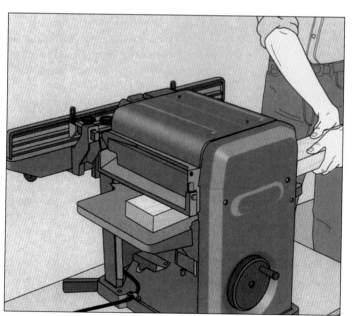

Planing Stock

Feeding the workpiece into the cutterhead

Set a cutting depth up to 1⁄16 inch. Stand to one side of the workpiece and use both hands to feed it carefully into the machine, keeping the edges of the stock parallel to the planer table. Once the machine grips the board and begins pulling it across the cutterhead, support its trailing end to keep it flat on the table *(left)*. Then move to the outfeed side of the planer. Support the workpiece with both hands until it clears the outfeed roller. To prevent stock from warping, avoid passing only one face of a board through the machine; instead, plane the same amount of wood from both sides.

Ripping a Workpiece

Using the rip fence as a guide
Set the blade height about ¼ inch above the workpiece. Position the rip fence for the width of cut, then push the stock into the blade, pressing it against the fence with your left hand and feeding with both thumbs *(right)*. Stand to one side of the workpiece and straddle the fence with your right hand, making sure that neither hand is in line with the blade. Keep pushing the board until the blade cuts through it completely. To keep your hands from coming closer than 3 inches from the blade, complete the cut with a push stick. **(Caution: Blade guard partially retracted for clarity.)**

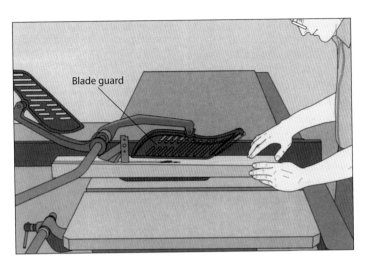

Blade guard

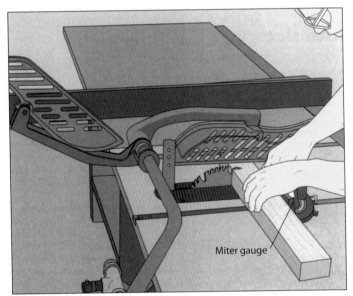

Miter gauge

Crosscutting Stock

Using the miter gauge
With the workpiece flush against the miter gauge, align the cutting mark with the blade. Position the rip fence well away from the end of the stock to prevent the cut-off piece from jamming up against the blade and kicking back toward you. Hook the thumbs of both hands over the miter gauge to hold the stock firmly against the gauge and flat on the table, then feed the board into the blade *(left)*. **(Caution: Blade guard partially retracted for clarity.)**

Sanding

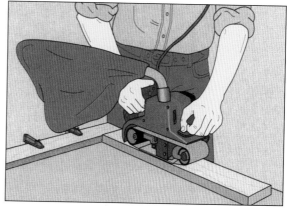

Using a sanding block
Clamp stop blocks to a work surface at both ends of the workpiece to hold it steady. Fit a sanding block with a piece of abrasive paper and sand the surface of the stock along the grain, applying even, moderate pressure *(above)*. Use long, smooth, overlapping strokes until the surface is smooth. Repeat with a finer-grit paper for a smoother finish. To prevent rounding the edges of the workpiece, keep the sanding block flat on its surface, and work up to—but not over—the edge.

Using a belt sander
Use a stop block to keep the workpiece from moving. Install a sanding belt and drape the power cord over your shoulder to keep it out of the way. With the sander parallel to the wood grain, turn it on and slowly lower it onto the surface, holding it firmly with both hands *(above)*. Move the machine back and forth with the same type of strokes you would use with a sanding block. To avoid gouging the surface, keep the sander flat and always moving; do not let the machine rest in one spot.

The Belt Sander as Planer

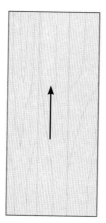

Smoothing a panel
If a planer is not available to even out the surface of glued-up panels, use a belt sander. The diagrams on the left illustrate the correct sequence of operations. First, slowly move the sander back and forth across the surface at a 45° angle to the wood grain *(far left)*. Be sure to cover the entire surface, but do not let the sanding drum run completely off the edges of the panel; this may round the corners. Next, make a second pass back and forth diagonally across the grain in the opposite direction *(center left)*. Finally, run the tool along the wood grain to remove any scratches left by the earlier sanding *(near left)*.

Carcase Construction

The basic box—or carcase—featured in this chapter has long been the starting point of many types of furniture. The earliest examples were simple coffers, nailed or pegged together, that served double-duty as chests or benches. Today, there are seemingly limitless variations on that same basic design. The smallest examples of carcase construction feature delicate pieces of highly figured, exotic woods, such as bird's-eye maple, rosewood, or Hawaiian koa, that are assembled with precise joints and delicate hinges to form jewelry boxes and silver chests. Larger but still compact boxes provide the framework for drawers.

Once assembled, the type of carcase examined in the pages that follow can be the basis for anything from a small dresser or tool chest to a floor-to-ceiling cabinet or a home-entertainment center. The later chapters in this book look at the subsequent steps—adding drawers, doors or legs—so as to turn the basic carcase into a finished piece of furniture.

Although carcases and drawers are designed to withstand different types and levels of stress in use, there are certain construction techniques that are applicable to both. Where appropriate, a cross-reference to the Drawers chapter will be included to direct you to a drawer-building technique that could prove useful for constructing carcases.

All carcases consist of four panels joined together to form a box. A key requirement is that the wood grain of all the panels run in the same direction. Since wood expands and contracts, especially across the grain, the panels will expand and contract together at the same rate, preserving the structural integrity of the box. Assembling a carcase with the grain of adjacent panels at right angles to each other virtually ensures that one of the panels will eventually split; when wood is ready to move, it is almost impossible to stop.

Much of the character and individuality of a particular carcase design derives from the method of assembling the panels. There are a great many types of corner joints you can use; some of the most common include dovetails, lock miters, rabbets, miter-and-spline joints, biscuit joints, and box and finger joints. Because dovetail joints are highly regarded for their strength and beauty in solid wood, one variety—the hand-cut through dovetail—is featured in this chapter *(page 29)*. It can also be cut more quickly with a jig as shown in the Drawers chapter *(page 82)*. In the eyes of many woodworkers, a well-made hand-cut dovetail joint is visible proof of the cabinetmaker's competence.

For plywood carcases, rabbet *(page 36)* or biscuit joints—also known as plate joints—*(page 38)* are better choices. Both offer pretty much the same strength as dovetail joints and, although less esthetically pleasing, they are quick and easy methods of assembly. The convenience factor becomes a major consideration if you are faced with producing a large number of carcases.

Drawers, shelves and a veneered plywood back panel transform a typical carcase into an elegant bookcase. The drawers run along fixed shelves set into dadoes cut in the side panels.

Using biscuit joints to assemble panels offers two very appealing benefits: strength and ease of assembly. A biscuit joiner cuts semicircular grooves into mating panels. The slots are filled with glue and biscuits of compressed beech, then the panels are butted together to form a perfect joint.

Lamello
Standard 10

Anatomy of a Carcase

Whether it is a box that will house a couple of drawers and a shelf or a china cabinet destined to grace your dining room, the carcase you build will feature many of the basic elements illustrated below. First, it will have four sides, or panels, which are usually the same width and thickness. Another requirement is that parallel panels must have the same dimensions.

Although a panel can be made from a single piece of lumber, it is generally less expensive to glue narrower boards edge-to-edge to form the wide surface *(page 22)*. Once glued up, the panels are planed, jointed on one edge, cut to size, and then their surfaces are sanded. A third option—one which combines the economy of glued-up panels and the ease of solid lumber—is to use hardwood plywood, which can be made to look like solid wood, by the addition of a banding along exposed edges *(page 41)*. Constructing carcases from plywood does

This simple carcase-framed cabinet features edge-glued panels of ash and rabbeted corner joints cut on a table saw. A fixed upper shelf is set in dadoes cut into the side panels; a lower adjustable shelf rests on hidden supports.

Panel
Used to form the top, bottom and sides of the carcase. May be a single piece of plywood or solid lumber, but panels are more commonly made from smaller boards glued edge to edge; dowels may be used to help with alignment. Individual boards can be of varying widths, but are usually 2 to 5 inches wide.

Corner joint
Secures the ends of the panels together; rabbet joint is shown, but dovetail and plate joints are also popular choices.

Back
Usually ¼-inch plywood piece nailed and glued into a rabbet routed along back edge of the panels.

Shelving
May be plywood or single piece of wood, but often made from edge-glued boards. Fixed shelves are glued in dadoes routed on the inside surfaces of side panels; adjustable shelves rest on supports.

have its disadvantages, however. It reduces your flexibility when it comes to the joinery; dovetails, for example, simply will not work. It also rules out such esthetic possibilities as creating attractive grain patterns on the panels by edge gluing carefully matched boards.

If you plan to add edge banding or install shelves *(page 43)*, you must anticipate those steps before gluing the panels together. For shelves, you will need to rout

dadoes or bore dowel holes on the inside surfaces of the side panels.

For more detail on the cutting, jointing, sanding and other procedures necesssary to prepare boards and panels, refer to "Cabinet Construction" on page 14. Of the many joinery methods that can be used to connect the panels of a carcase, this chapter focuses on three of the most common: the hand-cut through dovetail joint, the plate joint, and the rabbet joint.

Corner Joints

Through dovetail joint
Tapered pins on one panel interlock with angled tails of the other and offers a large gluing surface. For best appearance, pins are usually cut at the ends of the top and bottom panels; tails are sawn at ends of the side panels. Strong, decorative joint for solid lumber; not recommended for plywood. Good choice when featuring joinery as an element of design.

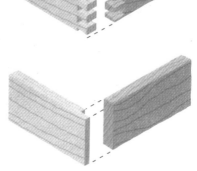

Plate or biscuit joint
Biscuits of compressed wood fit into slots in the mating boards; glue swells the biscuits, strengthening the joint. To conceal end grain when viewed from the side of carcase, slots are usually cut into end grain of top and bottom panels and into mating faces of side panels. Strong joint for solid lumber or plywood. Not decorative but quick and easy to make.

Rabbet joint
Edge of one board fits into rabbet cut in the mating board. To conceal end grain of top and bottom panels, the rabbets are normally cut into the side panels. Strong joint for solid lumber or plywood. Also used to join carcase back to panels. Not as decorative as a through dovetail, but not as strong and much simpler to make.

Edge banding
Decorative veneer commercially available but can be made in the shop; glued to exposed edges of plywood panels and shelves.

Making Wide Panels

Most woodworkers make up the wide panels for a carcase by gluing boards together edge-to-edge. Building a carcase this way is not a matter of cutting costs at the expense of strength. Panels of edge-glued boards are every bit as strong as a single piece of lumber. In fact, a proper glue joint provides a sturdier bond than the fibers of a piece of wood.

Follow the steps detailed below and on the following pages to assemble panels. Apart from a supply of glue and an assortment of clamps, all you need is a level work surface or a shop-built glue rack *(page 26)*. To help keep the boards aligned, some woodworkers also use dowels *(page 27)*.

Selecting your wood is an important part of the process. Do not buy green wood or stock that is cupped or twisted, and avoid using wood with a high moisture content, which can adversely affect the glue. Instead, buy lumber that has been dried in a kiln. If you are working from rough stock, begin preparing boards by jointing a face and an edge, then planing the other face. Next, crosscut the boards, leaving them roughly 1 inch longer than their finished length, and joint an edge of each piece. Rip the stock so that the combined width of all the boards exceeds the finished width of the panel by about 1 inch, then joint the cut edges.

Edge-glued boards should create the illusion of a single piece of wood rather than a composite. Experiment with the boards in different configurations to produce a pattern that is visually interesting, but make sure that the grain runs in the same direction on all of the pieces.

Edge Gluing

Arranging the boards

Set two bar clamps on a work surface and lay the boards on them. Use as many clamps as necessary to support the boards at 24- to 36-inch intervals. To keep the bars from moving, place them in notched wood blocks *(inset)*. Use a pencil to mark the end grain orientation of each board as shown, then arrange the stock on the clamps to enhance their appearance *(photo above)*. To minimize warping, arrange the pieces so that the end grain of adjacent boards runs in opposite directions. If the grain is difficult to read, dampen or sand the board ends to make it show up more definitely. Once you have a satisfactory arrangement, align the stock edge-to-edge and use a pencil or chalk to mark a triangle *(right)*. This will help you correctly rearrange the boards if you move them prior to final assembly.

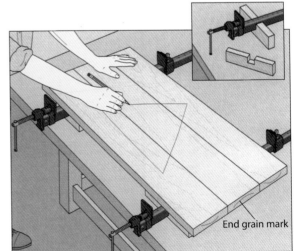

End grain mark

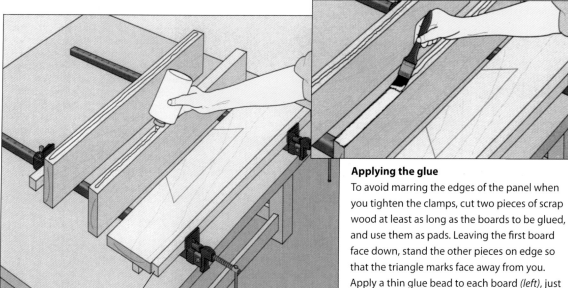

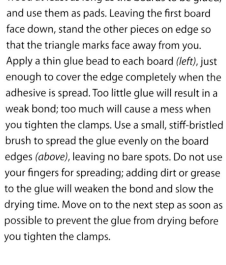

Wood pad

Applying the glue

To avoid marring the edges of the panel when you tighten the clamps, cut two pieces of scrap wood at least as long as the boards to be glued, and use them as pads. Leaving the first board face down, stand the other pieces on edge so that the triangle marks face away from you. Apply a thin glue bead to each board *(left)*, just enough to cover the edge completely when the adhesive is spread. Too little glue will result in a weak bond; too much will cause a mess when you tighten the clamps. Use a small, stiff-bristled brush to spread the glue evenly on the board edges *(above)*, leaving no bare spots. Do not use your fingers for spreading; adding dirt or grease to the glue will weaken the bond and slow the drying time. Move on to the next step as soon as possible to prevent the glue from drying before you tighten the clamps.

Shop Tip

Two ways to spread glue

To spread a glue bead quickly and evenly, use a rubber-based printer's brayer, available in a variety of sizes at art supply stores. To clean the roller after use, roll it repeatedly over a scrap board. For a shop-made glue spreader, use a 6-inch length of ½-inch dowel as a handle to hold a 2-inch section of a broken or worn hacksaw blade. Use a backsaw or band saw to cut a shallow slot in one end of the dowel, making it thin enough to hold the blade section snugly. Fit the blade teeth-side-out into the slot.

Tightening the clamps

Set the boards face down and line up their ends, making sure that the sides of the triangle align. Tighten the clamps under the boards just enough to butt them together, checking again for alignment. Avoid overtightening the clamps or the boards may buckle up at the joints. Place a third clamp across the top of the boards, centering it between the two underneath. Finish tightening all of the clamps in turn *(right)* until there are no gaps between the boards and a thin bead of glue squeezes out of the joints.

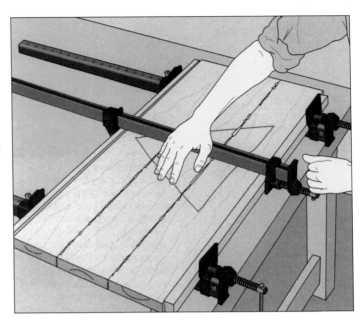

Leveling the boards

For adjacent boards that do not lie perfectly level with each other, use a C clamp to hold them in alignment. Protecting the boards with wood pads, center the clamp on the joint near the end of the stock; place a strip of wax paper under each pad to prevent it from sticking to the boards. Then tighten the clamp until the boards are level *(left)*. Refer to the manufacturer's instructions for the glue's drying time. If you are short of clamps, mark the time on the panel so that you can move on to the gluing of the next panel as soon as possible.

Wood pad

Removing the excess glue

Use a plastic putty knife to remove as much of the squeezed-out glue as possible before it dries. The moisture from glue left on the surface will be absorbed by the wood, causing swelling and slow drying; hardened adhesive can also clog sandpaper, dull planer knives and repel wood stain. Once the glue has dried, remove the clamps from the top of the boards, and use a paint scraper to remove any squeeze-out that remains *(right)*. Remove the lower clamps, then prepare the panel for joinery by planing it, jointing an edge, and cutting the piece to its finished dimensions. Use a belt sander to smooth the surfaces that will be hard to reach once the carcase is assembled.

Shop Tip

Preventing clamp stains
The metal bar of a clamp can be stained by adhesive that drips during gluing operations. Dried glue can also interfere with the ratcheting action of some clamps. To eliminate the problem, use a hacksaw or band saw to cut a roll of wax paper into 2-inch-wide mini-rolls. Then, each time you apply a clamp, tear off a strip of paper to wrap over or under the bar.

Glue Rack

A shop-built rack made from two sawhorses provides a convenient way to hold the clamps for gluing up a panel. To build the jig, remove the cross piece from your sawhorses. Cut replacements the same width and thickness as the originals, making them at least as long as the boards that you will be gluing.

Use a hand saw or a band saw to cut notches along one edge of each cross piece at 6-inch intervals. Make the cuts wide enough to hold a bar clamp snugly and deep enough to hold the bar level with the top of the cross piece. You can also cut notches to accommodate pipe clamps, but bar clamps are stronger.

To use the glue rack, seat at least two bar clamps in the notches so that the boards

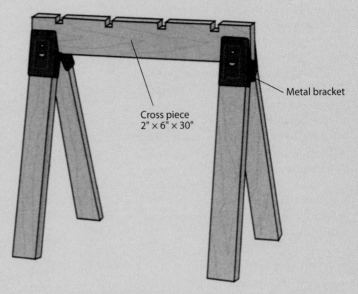

Metal bracket

Cross piece
2" × 6" × 30"

to be glued are supported at least every 24 to 36 inches. The rest of the operation is identical to edge gluing boards on a work surface as shown on the preceding pages.

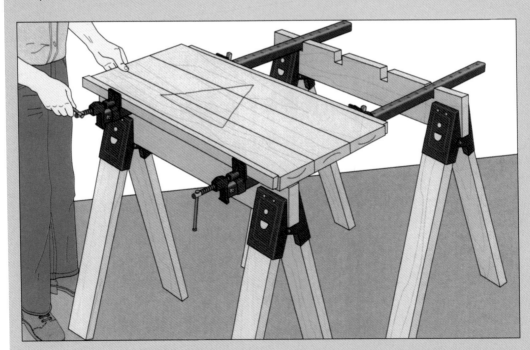

Dowels: an Aid to Alignment

Many woodworkers use dowels to help with the alignment of boards in a panel. One of the problems in using this technique is that the wood pins have to be precisely centered on the edges of the boards to be joined. In the photo at left, location points have been made for the dowels—one about 3 inches from each end of the boards and one in the middle. A line is then scribed across the points with a cutting gauge set to one-half the thickness of the stock. The lines intersect at the center of the board edges, guaranteeing perfect placement of the dowels.

Boring the dowel holes

Locate points for dowels on the board edges (*photo above*). To avoid splitting boards with the pins, use grooved dowels that are no more than one-half as thick as the stock. Fit a drill with a bit the same diameter as the dowels, then wrap a strip of masking tape around the bit to mark the drilling depth, which should be slightly more than one-half the length of the dowels. Keep the drill perpendicular to the board edge as you bore each hole (*right*), withdrawing the bit when the masking tape touches the stock. (Although the drill press can also be used to bore the holes, keeping longer boards steady on the machine's table may prove difficult.)

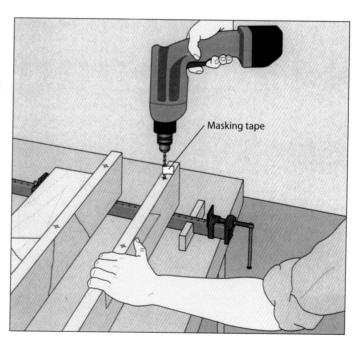

Masking tape

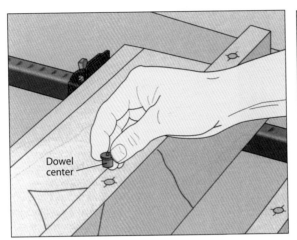

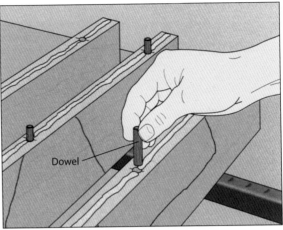

Pinpointing mating dowel holes

Insert a dowel center the same diameter as the dowels in each of the holes *(above)*, then set the boards flat on the clamps with the triangle mark facing you. Align the ends of the boards and butt the edge of the second board against that of the first. The pointed ends of the dowel centers will punch impressions on the wood, providing starting points for the mating dowel holes. Bore these holes to the same depth as before, then repeat the procedure for the third board.

Gluing up the boards

Apply glue to the board the same way as when edge gluing *(page 23)*. Then use a pencil tip to dab a small amount of adhesive in the bottom of each dowel hole. Avoid spreading glue directly on the dowels; they absorb moisture quickly and will swell, making them difficult to fit into their holes. Insert the dowels *(above)*, then tap them into final position using a hammer. Avoid pounding on the dowels; this may cause a board to split. Close up the joint, then tighten the clamps *(page 24)*. Remove the excess glue *(page 25)*.

Shop Tip

Inserting dowels with a depth gauge

To avoid the risk of splitting boards when inserting dowels, use this simple shop-made depth gauge. Rip a 9-inch-long board to a thickness that is exactly one-half the length of the dowels. Bore a hole that is slightly wider than the thickness of the dowels through the gauge near one end. Then place it around each dowel when you tap it into its hole. The dowel will be at the correct depth when it is flush with the top of the depth gauge.

Carcase Joinery

There are many ways of joining carcase panels together. The pages that follow will examine three of the most popular choices: dovetail, rabbet, and plate joinery. As shown in the photo at right, the interlocking pins and tails of a through dovetail joint give both solidity and distinctive appearance. Cutting such a joint with the traditional hand tools is considered a rite of passage for aspiring woodworkers. It requires skill and practice to perfect. The same joint can be executed using a router and a jig; that approach is demonstrated in the Drawers chapter *(page 82–83)*. You may also want to try the half-blind dovetail, which is examined on pages 84–86.

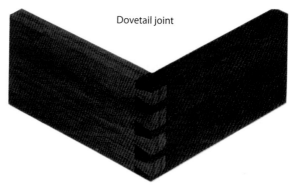

Dovetail joint

If you prefer somewhat simpler forms of joinery, try either the rabbet or the plate joint *(page 36–39)*. Both are ideal for joining plywood panels, which are not suited for dovetails.

Dovetail Joints

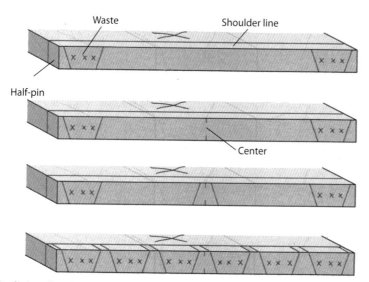

Waste   Shoulder line

Half-pin

Center

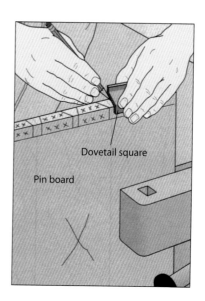

Dovetail square

Pin board

Outlining the pins

Mark the outside face of each panel with a big X, then set a cutting gauge to the thickness of the stock and scribe a line along the ends of the four panels to mark the shoulder of the pins and tails. The panels that will form the top and bottom of the carcase will be the pin boards. Secure each one in turn in a vise and use a dovetail square to outline the pins on the ends of the board as shown in

the sequence above. Start with half-pins at each edge, making sure that the narrow ends of the pins are on the outside face of the board. Next, outline the waste sections adjacent to the half-pins, then mark the center of the board end. Outline a pin at the center mark, then outline the remaining pins *(above, right)*, marking all the waste sections with Xs.

Cutting the pins

Secure the first pin board in a vise so that the outside face of the panel is toward you. Use a dovetail saw to cut along the edges of the pins, working from one side of the panel to the other. Some woodworkers prefer to cut all the left-hand edges first, then move on to the right-hand edges. For each cut, hold the panel steady and align the saw blade just to the waste side of the cutting line. Use smooth, even strokes, allowing the saw to cut on the push stroke *(right)*. Continue sawing right to the shoulder line, making sure that the blade is perpendicular to the line. Next, use a coping saw or a chisel to remove the waste between the pins. Repeat the procedure at the other end of the board and at both ends of the other pin board.

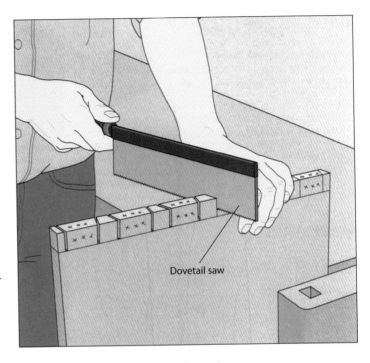

Dovetail saw

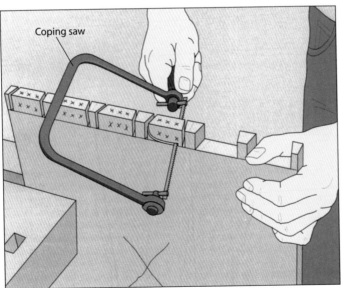

Coping saw

Removing the waste with a coping saw

Stand on the other side of the panel and begin cutting away the waste wood between the pins. At the side of each pin, slide a coping saw blade into the kerf and rotate the frame without striking the end of the board. Cut out as much of the waste as you can while keeping the blade about $\frac{1}{16}$ inch above the shoulder line. Cut *(left)* until you reach the kerf on the edge of the adjacent pin. Pare away any remaining waste with a chisel.

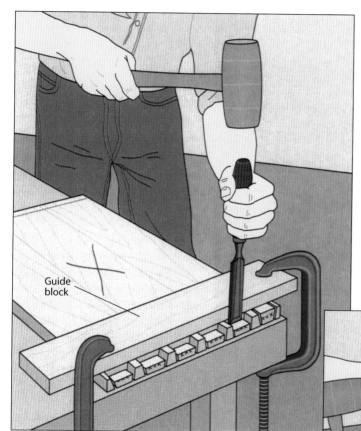

Removing the waste with a chisel

Set the panel outside face up on a work surface and clamp on a guide block, aligning its edge about 1/16 inch to the waste side of the shoulder line. Using a wood chisel no wider than the narrow side of the waste section, butt the flat side of the blade against the guide block. Hold the end of the chisel square to the face of the panel and strike it with a wooden mallet *(left)*, scoring a line about 1/8-inch-deep. Then turn the chisel toward the end of the panel about 1/8 inch below the surface of the wood and shave off a thin layer of the waste *(below)*. Continue shaving away the waste in this fashion until you are about halfway through the thickness of the panel, then move on to the next section. When you have removed all the waste from this side, turn over the panel, and work from the other side until the pins are all exposed.

Guide block

Final paring

With the panel outside face up, align the edge of a guide block with the shoulder line on the panel and clamp it in place. Butt the flat side of a chisel against the block, and using your thumb to hold the blade vertical, gently tap on the handle to pare away the final sliver of waste *(right)*. Repeat the process between the other pins until there is no waste beyond the shoulder line.

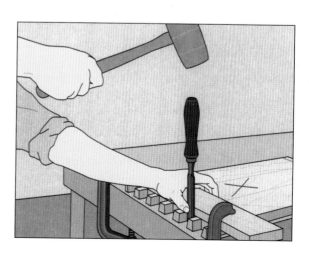

Preparing to outline the tails

Set one of the tail boards outside face down on a work surface and clamp a guide block on top of it with the edge of the block flush with the shoulder line. Then hold the end of one of the pin boards against the guide block with its outside face away from the tail board. Fasten a handscrew to the pin board and use another clamp to hold it firmly in position *(right)*.

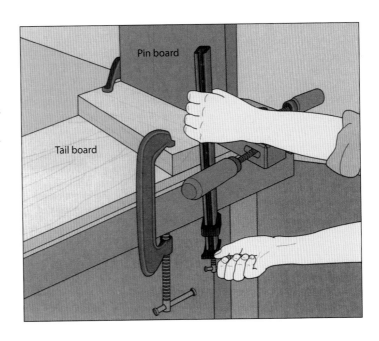

Marking the tails

Use a pencil to outline the tails *(left)*, then remove the clamps and use a combination square to extend the lines onto the end of the board. Mark the waste sections with Xs, then outline tails on the other end of the board and at both ends of the other panel.

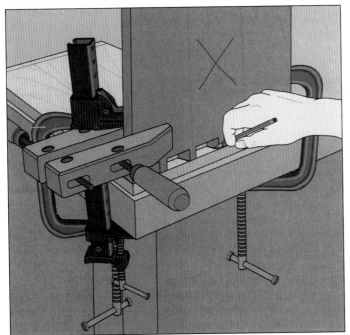

Cutting the tails and removing waste
Use a dovetail saw to cut the tails the same way you cut the pins. Some woodworkers find that angling the board, as shown, rather than the saw makes the cutting go easier. In either case, saw smoothly and evenly, and stop just a fraction of an inch before you reach the shoulder line. Remove the bulk of the waste with either a coping saw or a chisel, then pare away the final bits of waste down to the shoulder line.

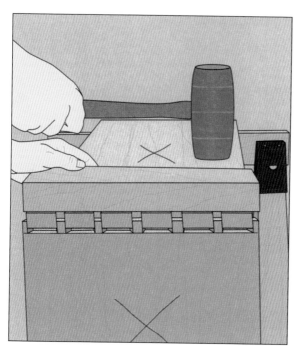

Dry-fitting the carcase
Before gluing up the carcase, assemble it to check the fit of all the joints. Stand one of the pin boards on a wood block, then align a mating tail board with it; support the other end of the tail board with a sawhorse. Press the joint together by hand as far as it will go, then tap the two ends the rest of the way into place, while protecting the workpiece with a scrap board. To avoid binding and damaging the pins, close the joint evenly along its whole length *(left)*. Join the other pin and tail boards the same way, tapping only on the tail board. The joints should be tight enough to require a little gentle tapping, but avoid using excessive force. If the joint is clearly too tight, mark the spot where it binds, then disassemble the panels and use a chisel to pare away a little more wood. Dry-fit the carcase again and make further adjustments, if necessary. If there is any gap between a pin and a tail, insert a thin wedge to fill it *(page 34)*. At this point, you will need to see to the other requirements of your project, such as installing a back panel *(page 40)* and edge banding *(page 41)*, if desired, then preparing the sides for shelves *(page 43)* or drawers. Once that is done, glue up the carcase.

Gluing up the carcase

To apply proper pressure when tightening the clamps, use four wood pads specially notched for dovetail joints. Make the pads the same length as the carcase panels are wide, and cut away little triangular notches so that the wood will only make contact with the tails and not exert pressure on the pins. Apply a thin bead of glue on the faces of the pins and tails that will be in contact when the joints are assembled. Use a small, stiff-bristled brush to spread the glue evenly, leaving no bare spots. Assemble the carcase and install two bar clamps across the faces of each of the pin boards in turn. Tighten the clamps a little at time *(right)* until a little glue squeezes out of the joints. Remove the excess glue, and keep the clamps in place until the glue is dry.

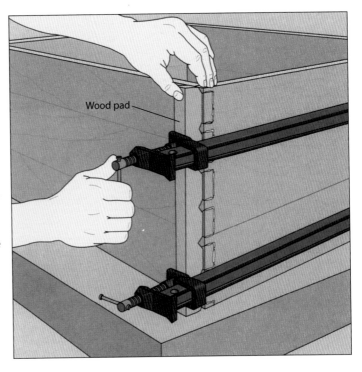

Wood pad

Shop Tip

Dealing with a defective dovetail

Even a slight error in cutting dovetails can result in a small gap between a pin and a tail. If the gap is small, fill it with a thin triangular chip of veneer or a wood shaving cut from the panel stock. To make the wood chip less obvious, cut it so that its grain will run in the same direction as that of the pins. Use a dovetail saw to straighten out or deepen the gap, if necessary. Apply a little glue in the gap and insert the chip, which should fit snugly.

Carcase-Squaring Blocks

Unless you are installing a back panel on a carcase, it can be difficult to keep the four sides square during glue up. A shop-made carcase-squaring block *(right)* placed on each corner will help a great deal. For each block, cut a piece of ¾-inch plywood into an 8-inch square. Fit a drill press or an electric drill with a 2-inch-diameter hole saw or circle cutter, then bore an opening in the center of the block. (The hole will prevent glue squeeze-out from bonding the block to the carcase.) Next, outfit your table saw with a dado head that is the same width as

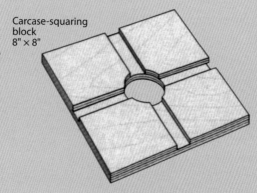

Carcase-squaring block
8" × 8"

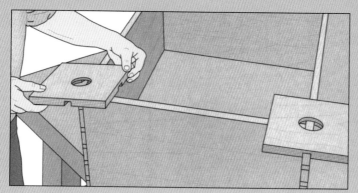

the thickness of the stock, and cut two grooves at right angles to one another, intersecting at the center of the block.

To use the jig, apply the glue and assemble the carcase, then fit a block over each corner *(left)*, centering the hole at the point where two panels join. Make sure that the dadoes on the blocks fit snugly around the edges of the panels. Install and tighten the clamps.

Shop Tip

Checking a carcase for square

To prevent clamp pressure from pulling a carcase out of square during glue up, measure the diagonals between opposite corners immediately after tightening the clamps. The two results should be the same. If they are not, the carcase is out-of-square. To correct the problem, loosen the clamps, then slide one jaw of each clamp away from the joint at opposite corners as shown.

Tighten the clamps and check again for square, shifting the clamps as necessary until the carcase is square.

Rabbet Joints

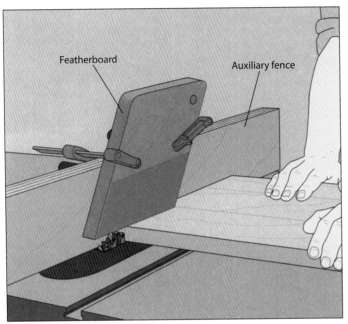

Featherboard

Auxiliary fence

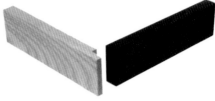

Quick and easy to cut and assemble, the rabbet joint is useful for both solid wood and plywood carcases. The joint is made up of a board or panel that fits into a rabbet cut on its mating piece. The width of the rabbet should be equal to the thickness of the stock. In a carcase, the joint is best cut into the side panels so that the end grain of the top and bottom will be covered. Although stronger than simple butt joints, rabbet joints usually require screws or nails for reinforcement.

Cutting the rabbets

Mark a cutting line for the width of the rabbet on the leading edge of one side panel. Then, install a dado head slightly wider than the rabbet and lower it below the table. Screw an auxiliary wood fence to the saw's rip fence and mark the depth of the rabbet on it; the depth should be one-half the thickness of the stock. With the metal fence clear of the dado head, position the auxiliary fence over the table opening. Turn on the saw. Raise the blades slowly into the wood up to the depth line. Turn off the saw and line up the panel and auxiliary fence for cutting the rabbet. Clamp a featherboard to the fence above the dado head to hold the panel securely against the table. Turn on the saw and make the cut *(above)*, then repeat the process for the remaining rabbets in the side panels. **(Caution: Blade guard removed for clarity.)**

Shop Tip

Invisible nailer

To conceal nails driven into a carcase panel, use a blind nailer. The commercial device works like a mini-plane, lifting a thin wood shaving under which a nail can be driven. The shaving can then be glued right back down to hide the nail head. Set up the nailer following the manufacturer's instructions—usually for a 1/32-inch-thick shaving. And practice on a scrap board before using the nailer on an actual workpiece. The shaving you raise must be long enough to let you drive the nail comfortably. A strip of tape will hold the shaving down while the glue is drying.

Gluing up the carcase

Dry-fit the carcase, then make any other necessary preparations, such as installing a back panel or preparing the sides for shelving. Then, apply a thin bead of adhesive in the rabbets and on the contacting surfaces of the top and bottom panels. Use a brush to spread the glue evenly, leaving no dry spots. Assemble the carcase and install two bar clamps across the top and bottom panels, protecting the workpieces with wood pads. Tighten the clamps a little at a time until glue starts to squeeze out of the joints. Reinforce the joints with screws about 1 inch from the edges of the top and bottom panels; for additional strength, drive more screws in the middle. If you wish to conceal the screw heads with wood plugs, bore holes in two stages using an electric drill fitted with two different bits. First, use a spade bit wide enough to make holes for the plugs; then switch to a twist bit slightly wider than the screw shanks for making clearance holes. Bore the clearance holes deep enough to reach the side panels; angle the drill slightly toward the inside of the carcase to increase the grip of the screws. Then, drive the screws into place *(right)*.

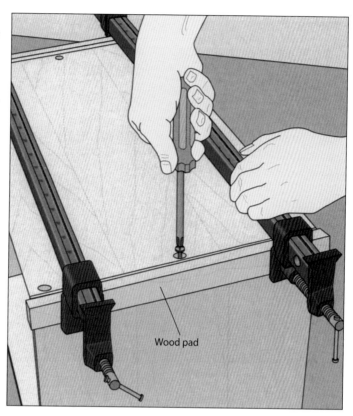

Wood pad

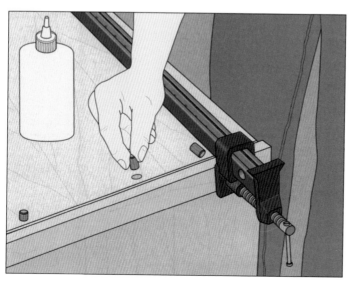

Installing wood plugs

To secure the plugs, apply a dab of glue to the screw heads, then insert a plug into each hole *(left)*, aligning the grain with that of the panels. Tap the plugs in place with a wooden mallet, then use a wood chisel to trim the projecting stubs flush with the surface of the panels. Finally, remove any excess glue *(page 25)*.

Plate Joints

Although it lacks the allure of hand-cut dovetails, the plate or biscuit joint has grown in popularity in recent years because of its strength and simplicity. The joint is cut with a plate joiner, shown in the photo at left. The tool works somewhat like a miniature circular saw, with a retractable blade that plunges into mating workpieces. Glue is applied and an oval-shaped biscuit of compressed beech is inserted into matching slots on each piece. The carcase is then assembled. Since the blade projects from the tool only while it is cutting, the plate joiner is very safe to use. Guide lines on the base plate of the machine make it a simple matter to align the slots in mating boards. The slots are cut slightly larger than the biscuits, permitting a small margin of error while still ensuring a properly aligned joint.

Marking the location of the joints

Identify the outside face of each panel with an X, then mark location points for the slots along each of the four corners. Start with one of the side panels outside face down on a work surface and hold the top panel at a 90° angle to it. Use a pencil to mark lines that overlap the face of the top piece and the end of the side panel about 2 inches in from each corner; make a third mark midway along the edge. Wider panels will require additional biscuits; in general, there should be one biscuit every 4 to 6 inches. Mark similar slot location points on the other three corners of the carcase.

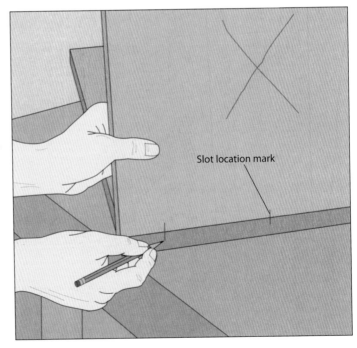

Slot location mark

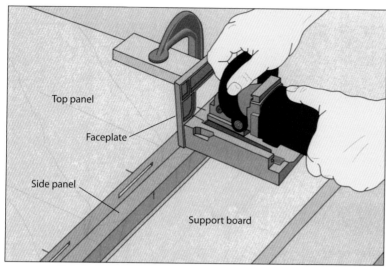

Top panel

Faceplate

Side panel

Support board

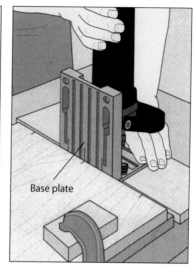

Base plate

Cutting the slots

Leaving a side panel outside face down on the work surface, set the top piece outside face up on top of it. Offset the ends of the two workpieces by an amount equal to the thickness of the stock. Make sure that mating slot location marks on the two panels are perfectly aligned. Protecting the top panel with wood pads, clamp the two workpieces in place and set in front of them a support board the same thickness as the stock. This setup will allow you to cut all the slots for one corner of the carcase without moving the panels. Follow the manufacturer's instructions for setting the depth of cut on the plate joiner; it usually depends on the size of biscuit being used. Resting the plate joiner on the support board, butt the machine's face plate against the end of the top panel and align the guide line on the faceplate with a slot location mark on the stock. Holding the joiner with both hands, cut a slot at each mark *(left)*. To cut the mating slots in the side panel, butt the joiner's base plate against the top panel and then align the center guide line on the base plate with a slot location mark on the top panel *(right)*. Follow the same procedure to cut slots at the other slot location marks.

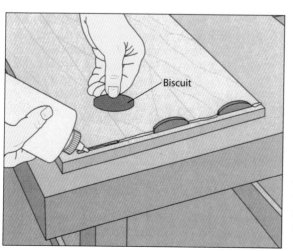

Biscuit

Gluing up the carcase

Once all the slots have been cut, dry-fit the panels and install a back panel if that is part of your design, or make ready for shelves or drawers. Then glue up the carcase: Set the side panels outside face down on a work surface, and squeeze a bead of glue into each slot and along the surface of the panels between the slots, inserting biscuits as you go *(left)*. Repeat for the top and bottom panels, this time omitting the biscuits. To prevent the wooden wafers from expanding before the panels are assembled, do the gluing up as quickly as possible, fitting the side panels on the bottom panel and then adding the top. Install two bar clamps across the top and bottom panels and tighten the clamps exactly as you would when gluing up a carcase with rabbet joints *(page 37)*.

Installing a Back Panel

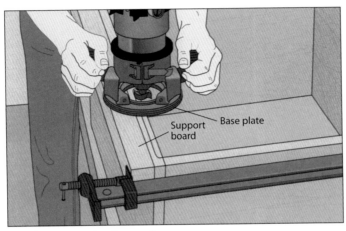

Support board   Base plate

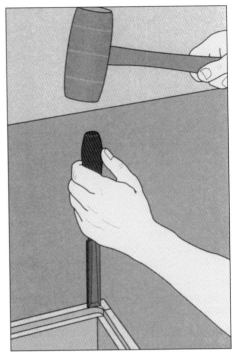

Routing a rabbet for the panel

Fit the panels together and set the carcase on a work surface with its backside facing up; install a bar clamp with a support board across the top and bottom panels, as shown. Install a ⅜-inch rabbeting bit with a ball-bearing pilot on your router, then set the depth adjustment to cut ¹⁄₁₆ inch deeper than the thickness of the back panel you will be installing. Starting at one corner, rest the router's base plate on the support board with the bit just clear of the workpiece. Grip the router firmly with both hands and turn it on, guiding the bit into the panel. Once the pilot butts against the stock, pull the router slowly toward the adjacent corner, keeping the base plate flat. When you reach the corner, turn the router off. Reposition the support board and cut rabbets along the edges of the three remaining panels in the same manner *(above)*.

Squaring the corners

Use a pencil and a straightedge to mark square corners in the rounded ends of the rabbets. Select a wood chisel that is wide enough to finish off the corners with two perpendicular cuts. At each corner, stand the tip of the chisel on the mark that runs across the grain, making sure that the bevel faces the inside of the carcase. Use a wooden mallet to strike the chisel *(above)*, cutting to the depth of the rabbet. Align the chisel with the other mark and strike the handle again. (Making the cut with the grain first may cause the panel to split.)

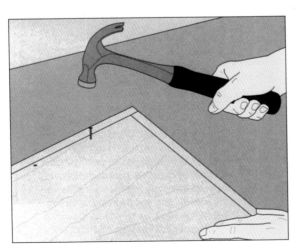

Installing the panel

Cut a piece of plywood to fit snugly into the rabbets on the back of the carcase. Glue up the carcase and, at the same time, apply a thin glue bead along the rabbets for the back panel and on the contacting surfaces of the plywood. Spread the glue evenly, set the panel in position, then use small nails to secure it at 4-inch intervals *(left)*.

Edge Banding

Edge banding is the usual way of concealing the visible edges of plywood panels and shelves; it creates the illusion that the carcase is made exclusively of solid wood. You can choose one of two options: Commercial edge banding, shown on page 42, is available in a wide variety of wood types, colors, and thicknesses. Installing it is simply a matter of cutting off the lengths you need from a roll, setting the banding in place and heating it with a household iron to melt the adhesive that bonds it to the surface of the wood.

Although somewhat more painstaking to apply, shop-made edge banding offers several advantages over the store-bought solution. You can make it from any available wood species and cut it to whatever thickness you choose; ⅛-inch-thick banding is typical. The shop-made variety is also less expensive—a consideration if you plan to use a lot of banding.

Shop-Made Edge Banding

Applying the banding

Use the table saw to cut thin strips of edge banding from a board; be sure to use a push stick to feed the stock into the blade. Make the strips slightly longer than the panel and at least as wide as the panel is thick. Grip the panel at each end in a handscrew, then clamp the handscrews to a work surface so that the front edge of the workpiece faces up. Then apply a thin glue bead to the edge of the panel and use a small, stiff-bristled brush to spread the adhesive evenly. Center the banding along the panel's edge; to hold it flat while the glue dries, tape it very firmly at 2-inch intervals. Use as many strips of tape as necessary to eliminate any gaps between the banding and the edge of the panel.

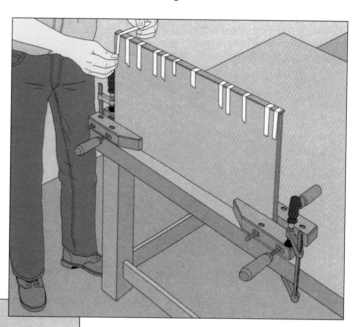

Trimming excess banding

Once the glue has dried, trim any edge banding that projects beyond the panel edges. Fit a router with a flush-cutting bit, then rest the machine's base plate on the panel edge with the bit just clear of the excess banding. Holding the router firmly with both hands, turn on the motor and guide the bit into the excess banding. Once the bit's pilot butts against the panel, guide the router slowly against the direction of bit rotation to the opposite end of the workpiece. Make sure that the base plate and the pilot remain flush with the panel. Lightly sand the edges and ends of the banding to remove any remaining unevenness.

Self-Adhesive Banding

Applying the edge banding

Set a household iron on high (without steam) and allow it to heat up. Meanwhile, apply clamps to hold the panel upright, and cut a strip of banding slightly longer than the edge to be covered. Set the banding adhesive-side down along the panel edge. Holding the banding in place with one hand, run the iron slowly along the panel edge, pressing the trim flat. The heat of the iron will melt the glue and join the banding to the panel. Keep the iron moving; resting it on one spot for more than a few seconds will leave scorch marks.

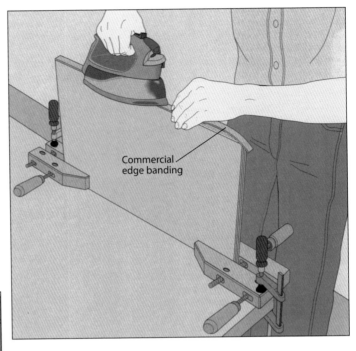

Commercial edge banding

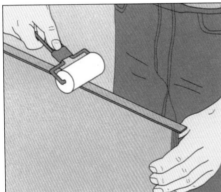

Flattening out the trim

Applying even pressure, run a small hand roller back and forth along the length of the edge banding to smooth it out and bond it firmly to the panel edge. Shave off any excess banding with a laminate edge trimmer or a router *(page 41)*.

Shop Tip

Springboard for clamping edge banding

For thick edge banding, it may be necessary to clamp the banding to a panel edge while the glue dries. For a typical panel, you might need three or four bar clamps; a single clamp will suffice, however, if you use a shop-made springboard. To make the device, cut a gentle curve—¼-inch-deep at its center—from one edge of a 2-inch-wide board the same length and thickness as the panel. Center the panel on a bar clamp and set the concave edge of the springboard against the edge banding. Use a wood pad to protect the panel. Tighten the clamp until the springboard flattens against the banding.

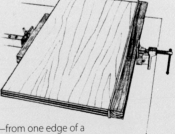

Shelving

Adding shelves to a carcase is one way to turn a simple wood box into a useful piece of furniture. The simplest method for installing shelves is to bore two parallel rows of holes in the side panels of the carcase and insert commercially available plastic or metal shelf supports. The two alternatives shown in this chapter require a little more preparation, but they have a payoff in that there are no visible shelf supports to mar the appearance of the finished piece. Like commercial shelf hardware, hidden supports *(below and page 44)* are adjustable; the difference is that they rely on narrow wood strips recessed in rabbets cut into the underside of the shelves, and this makes them all but invisible.

For fixed shelves *(page 45)*, you have to rout dadoes on carcase sides. The shelves are then glued permanently in place when the carcase is assembled.

Shelf-drilling jig

Many woodworkers use commercial shelf-drilling jigs to help with the job of boring parallel rows of holes. Clamped to the edge of the panel, the jig ensures that the corresponding rows are perfectly aligned. The jig in the photo allows you to bore holes at 1-inch intervals any distance from the edges of the panel. For most projects 2 inches in from the edges is typical.

Hidden Adjustable Shelf Supports

Shelf support

Making and installing the shelf supports

Bore holes for the shelf supports using a commercial jig. After the carcase is assembled, make two supports per shelf. For each of them, cut a thin strip of wood about 1 inch longer than the gap between the rows of holes; make the strip wide enough to hold a dowel at each end. To mark positions for the dowels, insert a dowel center into each of two parallel holes, then press the wood strip against the points. Use the indentations for the dowel centers as starting points for boring the holes. Make the holes in the shelf-support pieces the same depth as the holes in the side panels. Glue dowels into the shelf supports, and when the adhesive has dried, install them on the side panels at the height that you want the shelf to rest.

Making and preparing the shelving

Use solid lumber, plywood or edge-glued boards *(page 22)* to make the shelving. Cut each shelf to the same width as the carcase panels and to a length equal to the distance between the side panels. Add edge banding to the visible edge of the shelf *(page 41)*, if desired. To conceal the supports, rout stopped rabbets in the shelf. Start by positioning the shelf on the supports and outlining their locations on the underside of the shelf. Using a wood pad to prevent any marring, clamp the shelf to a work surface. Fit a router with a rabbeting bit, then set the depth of cut to the width of the shelf supports. Gripping the tool firmly with both hands and resting its base plate on the shelf, rout each rabbet *(above)*, making as many passes as necessary to cut to the marked outline. Square the ends of the rabbets using a chisel *(page 40)*.

Installing the shelving

With the shelf supports at the desired height on the side panels, test-fit the shelf in the carcase *(above)*. Use a chisel to adjust the length, width, or depth of the stopped rabbets, if necessary, to ensure a perfect fit that completely hides the shelf supports.

Fixed Shelving

Preparing the carcase side panels

Set the side panels one on top of the other on a work surface, edges and ends aligned, and mark cutting lines for the dadoes on the leading edges of both panels. Make the width of the dadoes equal to the thickness of the shelf; the depth should be one-half the thickness of the side panels. Install a dado head on a table saw and align the cutting lines on one side panel with it. Crank the blades to the proper height for the depth of cut, then position the rip fence flush against the panel. Cut a test dado in a scrap board and adjust the width of cut if necessary. Clamp a featherboard to the fence above the dado head for added stability. To make the cut in each panel, turn on the saw and feed the panel into the dado head using the miter gauge and both hands *(right)*. **(Caution: Blade guard removed for clarity.)**

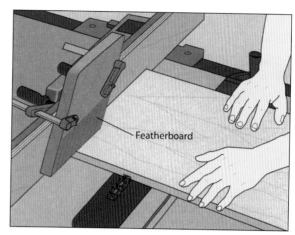

Featherboard

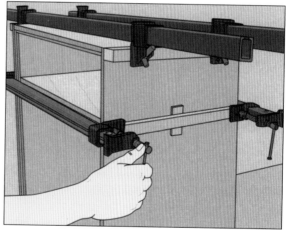

Making and dry-fitting the shelving

Use solid lumber, plywood or edge-glued boards *(page 22)* to make the shelving. Cut each shelf to the same width as the carcase panels and to a length equal to the distance between the side panels plus the depth of the dadoes. Add edge banding to the visible edge of the shelf *(page 41)*, if desired. To check the fit of the shelving, join the top and bottom panels of the carcase with one side panel, then fit the shelving into the dado *(above)*. Fit the other side panel on top. Adjust the length or width of the shelving, if necessary, to ensure a perfect fit.

Gluing up the carcase

Apply a thin glue bead into the dadoes in the side panels and on the contacting surfaces of the shelving while gluing up the carcase. Spread the glue evenly and then assemble the box as when dry-fitting. Clamp the corners of the carcase for dovetail joints *(page 34)* or for rabbet or plate joints *(page 36)*. For the shelving, install a bar clamp across each edge of the shelf, protecting the side panels with wood pads; place a ¼-inch-thick wood chip under each pad to focus some of the clamping pressure midway between the edges of the shelving. Tighten each clamp a little at a time until a thin glue bead squeezes out of each dado.

Frame-and-Panel Construction

Frame-and-panel joinery was invented about 500 years ago, probably by a frustrated medieval craftsman determined to find a better way to build cabinets than simply fixing boards together. It offers a solution to wood's tendency to warp and split.

Ever-changing moisture levels in the air cause wood to move, especially across the grain. As relative humidity rises, wood swells; as the moisture content falls, wood shrinks. The central heating found in most modern homes compounds the problem.

Frame-and-panel construction is designed to accommodate the movement of swelling and shrinking wood, resulting in furniture that is both strong and stable. In the typical piece shown on the two pages that follow, individual frame-and-panel assemblies are joined together to form a four-sided cabinet. Each assembly comprises two vertical members—stiles—and two or more horizontal rails, all locked together by any one of a variety of joints. These can include dowel, plate, miter-and-spline and lap joints. This chapter will show you how to use the haunched mortise-and-tenon *(page 50)* and the decorative cope-and-stick joint *(page 53)*.

The opening in the frame is filled by a "floating" panel, which sits in grooves cut in the rails and stiles. The panel is said to float because it is not glued in place. Rather, it merely fits in its grooves with room for

movement. If the panel were glued in place, the assembly might eventually split.

Panels are set into their surrounding frames without glue to minimize warping. But in addition to their structural function, panels also serve an esthetic role. They are often "raised"—that is, they have bevels cut around their edges. This not only makes them easier to fit into grooves, but also gives them decorative interest.

With one frame-and-panel assembled, you need only repeat the process and vary it slightly to build a cabinet *(page 61)*. Usually, two assemblies are joined together with side rails and panels, with the front assembly left open for a door.

As you will see in the pages that follow, frame-and-panel construction is a versatile furniture-building system. You can add a bottom panel to a cabinet *(page 62)*, then a top *(page 66)* and either fixed or adjustable shelving *(page 63)*. Installing molding *(page 71)* hides the connection between the frame and the top; it also adds a decorative flourish.

This clamping setup focuses pressure on the corner joints to lock together the components of a frame-and-panel assembly. While glue bonds the corners, no adhesive is applied in the grooves that hold the panel, allowing it to move as the wood expands and contracts.

Mounted upside-down in a table, a router fitted with a coping bit cuts a tongue at the end of a rail. Another bit will cut a matching groove into the stiles, making a solid and attractive cope-and-stick joint, one of the hallmarks of frame-and-panel construction.

Anatomy of a Frame-and-Panel Assembly

Despite their differences, the frame-and-panel assemblies that make up a typical cabinet have elements in common: Namely, frames made from rails and stiles, and panels that fit into grooves in the frame. Bottoms and tops are usually added, along with shelving in many cases. These components are typically made of edge-glued boards of the same stock used for the frame.

Individual cabinets will feature variations. In some instances, the sides will share stiles with the front and back assemblies with rails fitting into both the edges and the faces of the stiles. To provide access to the inside of the cabinet, the front frequently has a frame but no panel. Sometimes, a median rail is used to divide the opening into two discrete sections.

The two most common joints in frame-and-panel cabinets are the haunched mortise-and-tenon and the cope-and-stick. The haunched mortise-and-tenon offers greater gluing surface than the standard mortise-and-tenon, making it a very strong joint. The haunch also fills in the end of the groove cut into the stiles, eliminating the need for stopped grooves. The cope-and-stick joint provides comparable strength and adds its own decorative touch. The router bit that cuts the grooves for the panel also carves a decorative molding in the inside edges of the frame. Whatever the joint, cabinetmakers usually build frames from ¾-inch stock that is at least 2 inches wide; larger stock may also be used to suit the dimensions of a particular project.

Frame-and-Panel Joints

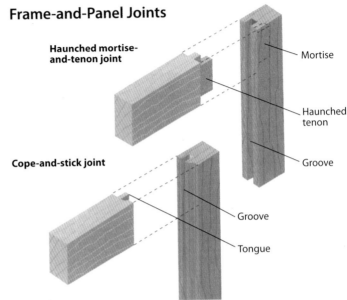

Haunched mortise-and-tenon joint

Mortise

Haunched tenon

Groove

Cope-and-stick joint

Groove

Tongue

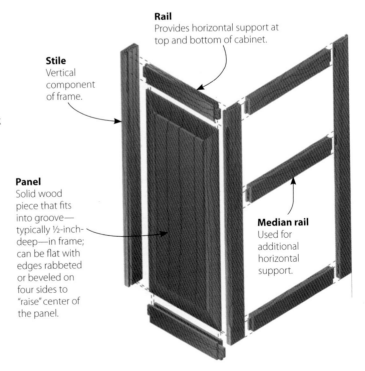

Rail
Provides horizontal support at top and bottom of cabinet.

Stile
Vertical component of frame.

Panel
Solid wood piece that fits into groove—typically ½-inch-deep—in frame; can be flat with edges rabbeted or beveled on four sides to "raise" center of the panel.

Median rail
Used for additional horizontal support.

48

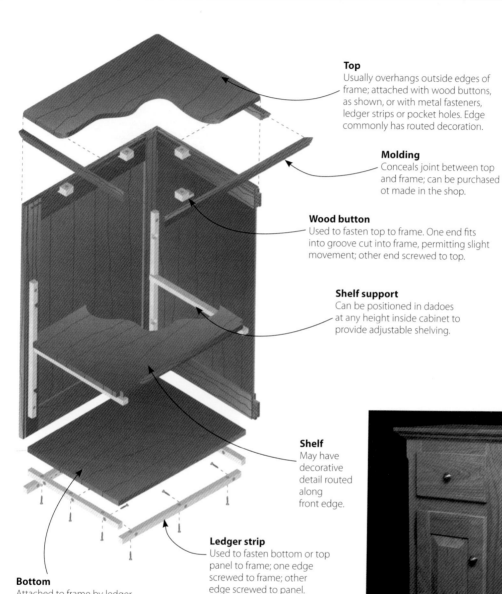

Top
Usually overhangs outside edges of frame; attached with wood buttons, as shown, or with metal fasteners, ledger strips or pocket holes. Edge commonly has routed decoration.

Molding
Conceals joint between top and frame; can be purchased ot made in the shop.

Wood button
Used to fasten top to frame. One end fits into groove cut into frame, permitting slight movement; other end screwed to top.

Shelf support
Can be positioned in dadoes at any height inside cabinet to provide adjustable shelving.

Shelf
May have decorative detail routed along front edge.

Bottom
Attached to frame by ledger strips or glued into groove cut in inside edges of frame.

Ledger strip
Used to fasten bottom or top panel to frame; one edge screwed to frame; other edge screwed to panel.

This frame-and-panel cabinet is held together by haunched mortise-and-tenon joints. The front has rails and stiles, but no panel. Instead, a median rail serves as a dividing line between the openings for a door and a drawer.

49

Making the Frame

Whether you will be using the standard mortise-and-tenon joint, the haunched version of that joint *(right, top)*, or the cope-and-stick joint *(right, bottom)*, calculate the number of rails and stiles you will need so you can cut them all to length and width at the same time.

For the haunched mortise-and-tenon and the cope-and-stick, you must cut a groove for the floating panel along the inside edges of the rails and stiles. The groove is typically ¼ inch wide and ½ inch deep, and the panel is cut to dimensions that allow ¼ inch of its edges to sit in the groove. If you opt for mortise-and-tenon joints, you also need to cut a haunched—or notched—tenon at the ends of each rail to accommodate the panel. For frames with no panels, such as the front of the case shown on page 61, you have to cut standard mortise-and-tenons. To produce this joint, follow the same procedures used in making the frame of a frame-and-panel door *(page 106)*. Whatever type of tenon you decide to make, cut it ¾ inch long and the same thickness as the groove in the stiles.

Haunched mortise-and-tenon joint

Cope-and-stick joint

Haunched Mortise-and-Tenon Joints

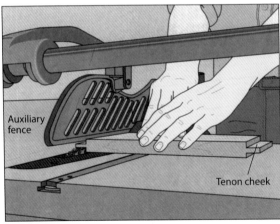

Auxiliary fence

Tenon cheek

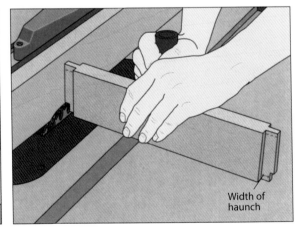

Width of haunch

Cutting the tenons in the rails

Install a dado head slightly wider than the length of the tenons on a table saw, then attach an auxiliary fence and raise the blades to cut a notch in it. Set the width of cut equal to the tenon length. To cut the tenon cheeks, butt the stock against the fence and the miter gauge, then feed it face-down over the blades. Turn the rail over and repeat the cut on the other side. Next, cut the tenon cheeks at the other end of the rail *(above, left)*. Position the fence to leave a haunch equal in width to the depth of the groove for the panel; set the height of the dado head to cut about ½ inch into the tenon. With the stock on its edge, use the fence and the miter gauge to guide it over the blades. Repeat to cut the haunch on the other side of the tenon *(above, right)*. For the rails of an assembly with no panel, cut standard tenons *(page 106)*, making the shoulders equal to the width of the notch you cut into the haunched tenons.

Planning the mortises in the stiles

First, evaluate the appearance of the boards for the stiles and arrange them on a work surface with their best sides facing down. For a four-sided cabinet, such as the one shown on page 61, set the stiles in their relative positions—one at each corner—and number them in sequence, beginning with the front left stile. This will help you rearrange the stiles should they get out of sequence. Next, mark the approximate locations of the mortises, putting Xs on the inside edges and the inside faces at the tops and bottoms of the stiles *(right)*. For stiles with a median rail, mark an additional X at the appropriate location on the edge of the stock.

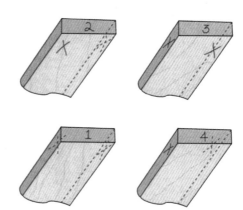

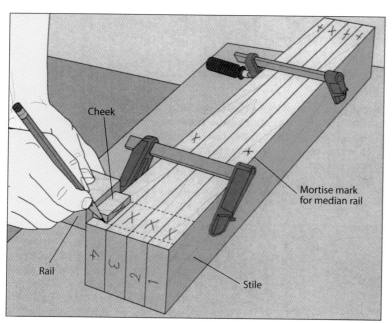

Cheek

Mortise mark for median rail

Rail

Stile

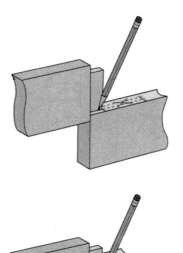

Outlining the mortises

Clamp the stiles together face to face, ends aligned. To mark the length of the mortises, use a rail with a standard tenon. Hold the cheek of the tenon flush against the edge of a stile so that the edge of the rail is aligned with the end of the stile. Outline the width of the tenon *(above, left)*. Then use a try square to extend the marks *(dotted lines in the illustration)* across all the stiles. Repeat at the other end and for any marks for median rails. To mark the width of the mortises, remove the clamps and hold the edge of the tenon

flush against the edge of the stile *(above right, top)*; repeat for the other stiles. Extend the marks along the edge of the stile *(dotted lines)*. To outline the mortises on the faces of the stiles, first mark the length by extending the lines across the edges of the stiles to the faces. For the width, hold the edge of the tenon flush against the marked face of the stile and outline the cheeks of the tenon on the stile *(above right, bottom)*. Extend the lines along the face *(dotted lines)*. Repeat for the other stiles.

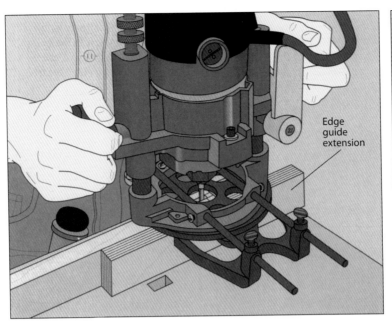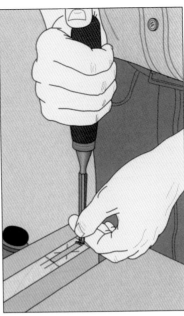

Edge
guide
extension

Routing the mortises

Secure a stile in a vise. Install a commercial edge guide on a plunge router, then screw onto the guide a wood extension as wide as the edge of the stile. Fit the router with a straight bit the same diameter as the width of the mortise you will be cutting, then set the cutting depth. Center the bit over the marks for the mortise and adjust the edge guide to butt the extension against the stile. Gripping the router firmly with both hands, turn it on and plunge the bit into the stock *(above, left)*. (If you are using a conventional router, carefully pivot the tool's base plate on the stock to lower the bit.) Guide the bit from one end of the mortise to the other. Make as many passes as necessary to cut the mortise to the required depth. Then, square the ends of the mortise using a chisel. Cut with the beveled edge of the chisel facing into the mortise *(above, right)*.

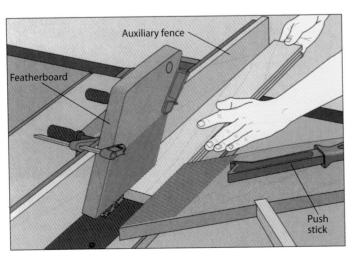

Auxiliary fence

Featherboard

Push
stick

Cutting the grooves

On the rails and stiles, mark locations for the grooves that will hold the panel. Then set up your table saw with an auxiliary fence and a dado head the same width as the groove. Place the edge of a rail or a stile on the table with the dado head aligned to run right along its middle, and adjust the fence to butt against the stock. Use featherboards to hold the workpiece against the fence while making the cut. To cut grooves on the faces of the stiles, keep the fence in the same position; use featherboards both above and to the sides of the stock *(left)*, and complete each pass with a push stick.

Cope-and-Stick Joints

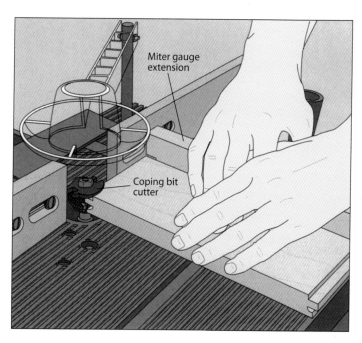

Miter gauge
extension

Coping bit
cutter

Making the cope cuts in the rails

Insert a coping bit—also known as a rail cutter—
with a ball-bearing pilot in a router, and mount
the machine in a router table. You will be cutting
tongues in the ends of the rails to fit into grooves
in the stiles. Butt the edge of the rail against the
bit and adjust the router's depth setting so that
the top of the uppermost cutter is slightly above
the stock. Position the fence parallel to the miter
gauge slot and in line with the edge of the bit
pilot. Make the cuts with a miter gauge fitted
with an extension and with the end of the stock
butted up against the fence (left).

Adjusting the height of the sticking bit

Install a sticking bit—or stile cutter—with a
ball-bearing pilot. This setup will, in a single
procedure, shape the edges of the stiles with a
decorative profile and cut grooves for the rails
and the panels. To set the cutting height, butt
the end of one of the completed rails against
the bit, then adjust the spindle setting on the
router so that one of the teeth on the bit is level
with the tongue on the rail (right). Align the
fence with the edge of the bit pilot.

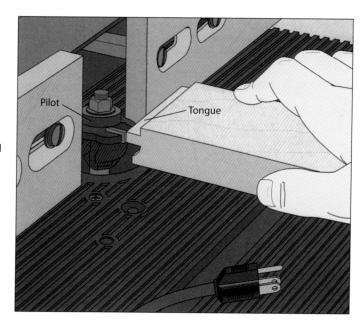

Pilot

Tongue

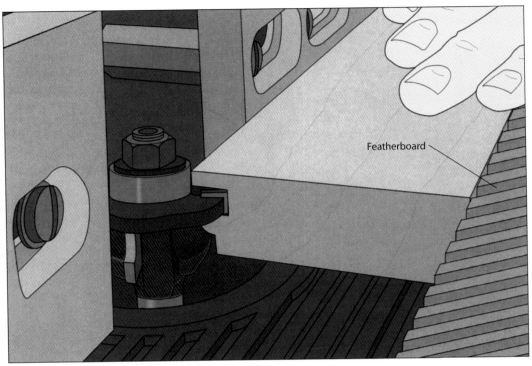

Featherboard

Cutting the stiles

To secure the workpiece, clamp a featherboard to the router table against the outside edge of the stile; for extra support, secure a second featherboard to the fence above the bit. When feeding the workpiece into the bit *(above)*, use a push stick to complete the pass.

Shop Tip

A shop-built miter gauge

If you do not have a miter gauge or if your router table is missing a slot, you can use a shop-made jig to guide stock accurately across the table. With the router table's fence aligned with the edge of the bit pilot, cut a board that will overhang the edge of the table by an inch or two when it is butted against the fence. Screw a short support piece to this board, countersinking the screws. Then, screw a third board to the underside of the support piece. This last addition will serve as a guide, running along the edge of the table. Before using the jig, cut a notch into it by running it past the bit.

Making the Panel

Panels to fit inside your frames can be made of either plywood or edge-glued boards *(page 22)*. To ensure that a panel will fit snugly in the grooves on the rails and stiles, but still have a little room to move as the wood expands and contracts, it is made substantially thinner on the edges than it is in the middle. The shape of such a so-called raised panel is achieved not by adding material at the center but by cutting away thickness at the edges.

There are several ways of making a raised panel, depending on the visual effect you wish to achieve. A common method, examined in this section of the book, involves beveling the edges of the panel with a table saw *(page 56)* or router *(page 58)*. Raised panel cutters for the router are availabe in several designs, including cove and ogee, and in various diameters. Make sure your router has at least 2 horsepower to make such a cut.

Before raising a panel, cut it to size. As shown below, this demands precision, since there is little room for play in the fit between the panel and the frame.

Although the design is different, beveling a panel's edges with a router *(top)* or a table saw *(bottom)* achieves the same effect: The center of the panel appears raised, while its edges are sufficiently narrow to fit into a groove in the frame.

Cutting the Panel to Fit

Miter gauge extension

Cutting a panel to size

Test-fit the rails and stiles of the frame, then measure the opening between them. For a frame assembled with cope-and-stick joints, measure the opening from the back, since the molding cut into the front of the frame makes precise calculation difficult. Add ½ inch to each of the dimensions for the opening to allow for the ¼ inch of stock along the edges of the panel that fits into the grooves in the rails and stiles *(inset)*. (The dotted lines in the illustration represent the actual edges of the panel; the solid lines represent the frame opening.) Cut the panel on the table saw, ripping first, then crosscutting. For the crosscut, screw a board to the miter gauge as an extension, then hold the panel firmly against the extension and push them together, feeding the stock into the blade *(left)*.

Making a Raised Panel with a Table Saw

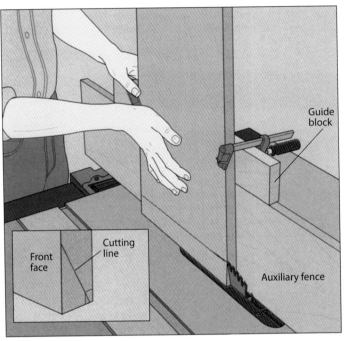

Guide
block

Front
face

Cutting
line

Auxiliary fence

Cutting the end grain

To set the blade angle, begin by marking a cutting line: Draw a ¼-inch square at the bottom corner, then mark a line from the front face of the panel through the inside corner of the square to a point on the bottom edge ⅛ inch from the back face *(inset)*. Rest the panel against an auxiliary wood fence and adjust the angle of the blade until it aligns with the marked line. Adjust the blade height until one tooth just protrudes beyond the front face of the panel, then clamp a guide block to the panel to ride along the top of the fence. Feed the panel into the blade, keeping it flush against the fence with your right hand while pushing it forward along with the guide block with your left hand *(left)*. Test-fit the cut end in a groove. If less than ¼ inch of the panel enters the groove, move the fence a little closer to the blade and make another pass. Repeat the cut at the other end of the panel.

Cutting with the grain

Set the panel on edge and feed it into the blade, keeping the back flush against the fence. Turn the panel over to cut the remaining edge *(right)*. Cutting into the end grain of the panel first—beveling the top and bottom before the sides—helps reduce tearout.

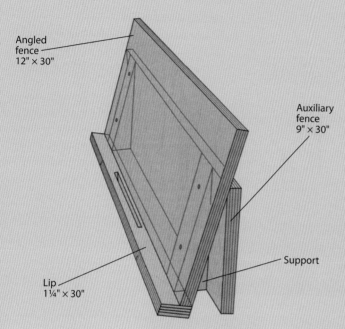

Angled
fence
12" × 30"

Auxiliary
fence
9" × 30"

Lip
1¼" × 30"

Support

A jig for cutting raised panels

To raise a panel on the table saw without adjusting the angle of the blade, use the shop-built jig shown at left. Refer to the illustration for suggested dimensions.

Screw the lip along the bottom edge of the angled fence, making sure to position the screws where they will not interfere with the blade. Prop the angled fence against the auxiliary fence at the same angle as the cutting line marked on the panel *(page 56)*. (Use a sliding bevel to transfer the angle.) Cut triangular-shaped supports to fit precisely in the space between the two fences, then fix them in place with screws.

To use the jig, position it on the saw table with the joint between the lip and the angled fence directly over the blade; ensure that the screws are well clear of the table opening. Slide the rip fence to butt against the jig's auxiliary fence, and screw the two together. Turn on the saw and crank the blade slowly up to cut a kerf through the lip. Next, seat the panel in the jig and adjust the height of the blade until a single tooth is protruding beyond the front of the panel. Make a test cut in a scrap board the same thickness as the panel, feeding it into the blade and then testing its fit in a groove. Adjust the position of the fence or blade, if necessary. Then cut the actual panel, beveling the sides with the end grain first *(left)*.

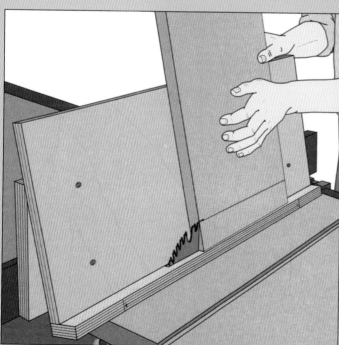

Making a Raised Panel with a Router

Bit pilot

Setting up the router

Fit a router with a panel-raising bit, then mount the tool in a router table. To ensure that the cutting width is uniform, position the fence parallel to the miter gauge slot and in line with the edge of the bit pilot. With the router turned off, place a scrap board along the fence and across the bit to check the position of the fence. The bit pilot should turn as the board touches it (*left*); adjust the fence's position, if necessary. Set the router for a ⅛-inch depth of cut.

Raising the panel

Lower the guard over the bit and turn on the router. To minimize tearout, cut into the end grain of the panel first, beveling the top and bottom before the sides. While running the stock past the bit, keep it flush against the fence with your left hand and push it forward with your right (*right*). The outside face of the panel must be down on the table. Turn off the router, then test-fit the cut end in a groove. If the panel sits less than ¼ inch deep into the groove, increase the cutting depth by ⅛ inch and make another pass.

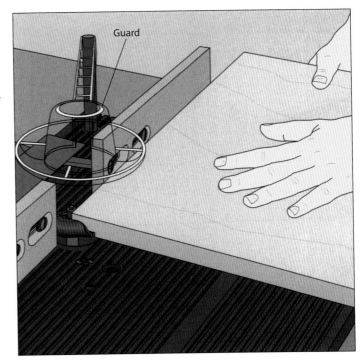

Guard

Putting the Panel in the Frame

Before gluing up the rails, stiles, and panel, take the time to dry-fit the parts. If the pieces do not fit perfectly, make final adjustments, as necessary. A slight shaving with a wood chisel will usually do the trick.

Since the individual frame-and-panel assembly is only one component of a piece of furniture, some further planning is required at this stage. You need to decide which methods you will use to install a bottom panel *(page 62)* and a top *(page 66)*. Some of the methods of installing those components require you to bore pocket holes in the rails or rout grooves in the rails and stiles. In either case, the stock will have to be prepared prior to gluing up.

A belt sander provides a quick and efficient start in smoothing the surfaces of a frame-and-panel. Here, the glued-up piece is clamped to a work surface for sanding the faces of the stiles and rails. The panel and the inside edges of the rails and stiles should be sanded prior to glue up.

Frame-and-Panel Construction

back to Basics

Assembling the Frame-and-Panel

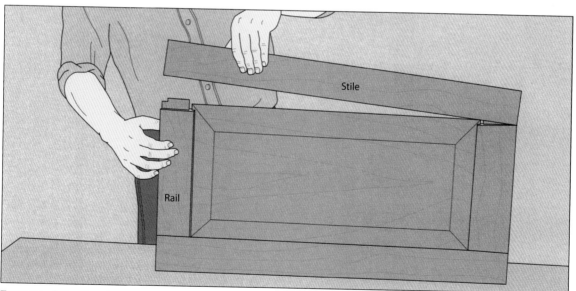

Stile

Rail

Test assembling the pieces

Join a rail and a stile, then seat the panel between them. Set the stile on a work surface, and add the second rail and stile *(above)*. Mark each of the joints using a pencil to help you in the final assembly, when you apply the glue. If any of the joints is too tight, mark the binding spots, disassemble the pieces and use a wood chisel to pare away some wood at the ill-fitting joint. Assemble the frame again. Once you are satisfied with the fit, disassemble the frame and sand any surfaces that will be difficult to reach once the assembly has been glued up.

Applying the glue

Make four clamping blocks, cutting them as long as the rails are wide and as wide as the stiles are thick. Lay out all of the components in their relative positions with their outside surfaces facing down. For mortise-and-tenon joints, squeeze glue into the mortises and on the tenon cheeks and shoulders; for cope-and-stick joints, apply glue to all the contacting surfaces. In either case, use just enough adhesive to cover the surfaces completely when it is spread out evenly *(right)*. Do not insert glue in the panel grooves; the panel must be free to move within these joints. After applying the glue, assemble the frame-and-panel.

Clamping blocks

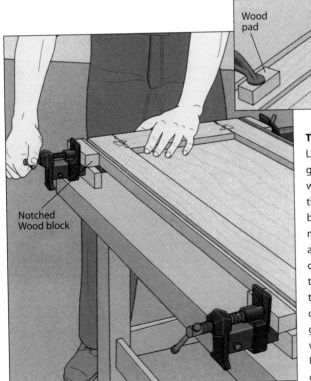

Wood pad

Scraper

Notched Wood block

Tightening the clamps

Lay two bar clamps on the work surface and place the glued-up assembly face down on them, aligning the rails with the bars. To keep the clamps from falling over, prop them up in notched wood blocks. Place clamping blocks between the stiles and the jaws of the clamps to avoid marring the stock and to distribute the pressure evenly along the joint. Tighten each clamp in turn just enough to close the joints *(left)*, then use a try square to make sure that the corners of the frame are at 90° angles. Continue tightening the clamps until a thin bead of glue squeezes out of the joints, checking for square as you go. Once the glue has dried, remove the clamps. Protecting the surface with a wood pad, clamp the assembly to a work surface. Use a paint scraper to remove any dried glue that remains on the wood, pulling the scraper along each joint *(inset)*.

Assembling a Frame-and-Panel Case

With a few variations, you can repeat the procedures shown on pages 59 and 60 to join individual frame-and-panel assemblies into a piece of furniture. A single frame and panel make up the back of a small cabinet. The front is put together in roughly the same way using mortise-and-tenon joints. On this side, however, there is no panel in the frame, but a median rail running between the stiles. In this situation, the rails and stiles can be joined with standard mortise-and-tenons *(page 106)*, rather than the haunched variety used for the other three sides.

The side assemblies are identical to the back, except for one feature: Instead of having stiles of their own, the sides fit into the stiles of the front and back assemblies. If you are using mortise-and-tenon joints, as in the piece of furniture shown below and on the following pages, the tenons of the side rails fit into mortises cut into the inside faces of the stiles; for cope-and-stick joints, tongues cut in the rails fit in grooves routed in the stiles. In both cases, the panels fit into grooves routed along the inside faces of the front and back stiles and the edges of the rails between them.

Gluing up a Cabinet

Putting the case together
Test-fit the case as you would when dry assembling a single frame-and-panel side *(page 59)*, then sand the inside surfaces of all the pieces. Apply glue to the joints—with the exception of the grooves that hold the panels—and make your final assembly: Set the back of the cabinet face down and fit the four side rails into its stiles. Install the two side panels in the groove in the back stiles and the inside edges of the side rails. Finally, put on the front, placing the mortises in the stiles over the haunched tenons on the side rails. Set the case upright and install four bar clamps running from front to back over the rails, protecting the surfaces of the stiles with wood pads. Tighten the clamps evenly *(right)* until a thin glue bead squeezes out of the joints. Use a measuring tape to check whether the case is square, measuring the distance between opposite corners; the two measurements should be equal. If not, install another bar clamp across the longer of the two diagonals, setting the clamp jaws on those already in place. Tighten the clamp a little at a time, measuring as you go *(below)* until the two diagonals are equal. Once the glue has dried, remove the clamps and use a paint scraper to remove any dried adhesive.

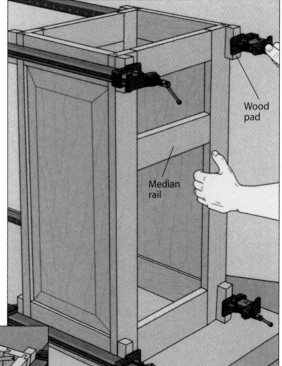

Wood pad

Median rail

Installing a Bottom Panel

There are several ways to install a bottom on a frame-and-panel case. One method that is popular among cabinet-makers calls for grooves along the inside faces of the bottom rails and the stiles prior to gluing up the individual frame-and-panel assemblies. The grooves can be made with a dado head on the table saw, and they should fall about 1 inch from the top edge of the bottom rails. They should be about ½ inch wide and half as deep as the thickness of the stock; stop the groove in the stiles at the point where the side rails butt up against them.

To install the panel, narrow its edges slightly with a plane, allowing the piece to fit snugly in the grooves, but not completely restricting its movement.

Another type of installation, shown below, relies on ledger strips, which are screwed to the bottom rails. With this approach, the bottom can be installed after glue up. Using either method, the bottom is made from the same stock used for the rest of the case. Make the width of the panel slightly narrower than its opening to allow for wood expansion.

Attaching the Panel

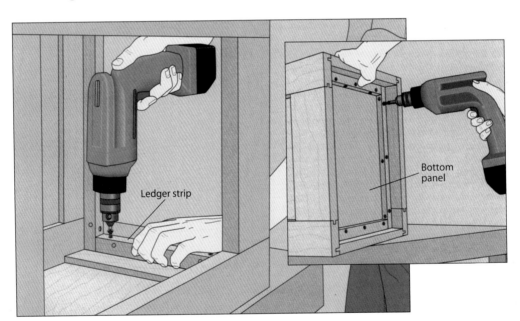

Ledger strip

Bottom panel

Installing ledger strips

Saw four 1-inch-square ledger strips to fit along the rails at the bottom of the cabinet, cutting them slightly short to make them easier to install. Bore two sets of holes in each strip: one in the center along one edge, for screwing the strip to the case, and another to the side of an adjacent edge for attaching the bottom panel. Bore the holes in two steps with two different brad-point bits: one bit slightly larger than the diameter of the screw heads for recessing the fasteners and another bit slightly larger than the diameter of the screw

shanks to provide clearance holes. (The wider hole will allow for movement.) Position the strips on the inside surface of a rail about 1 inch from its top edge and mark the positions of the screw holes with an awl. Bore a pilot hole for a No. 8 screw at each marked point, then use a drill fitted with a screwdriver bit to fasten the strips to the case *(above, left)*. To install the bottom panel, set the case on its back. Holding the panel flush against the strips with one hand, screw the bottom panel in place *(above, right)*.

Shelving

The number and placement of shelves in a frame-and-panel cabinet will depend on the use you have in mind for the furniture. If the cabinet will hold books, for example, you may need fewer shelves than if it will be the place for your compact discs.

Although some shelf-support systems can be put in place after the cabinet is glued up, a little advance planning will make the installation easier. First, choose between fixed and stationary shelves; each has its advantages.

Fixed shelves can add to the structural integrity of a case, but once installed they cannot be moved. One way to install permanent shelves is to mount cleats on the frame inside the cabinet and then screw the shelving to them. Fixed shelves can also be glued into dadoes routed in the frame before the cabinet is assembled.

While adjustable shelves do not add strength to a piece of furniture, they allow greater flexibility. As in simple carcase construction, adjustable shelves are commonly held in place with wooden dowel pins, plastic or metal shelf pins, or adjustable shelf standards. The method shown below and on the following pages uses corner strips and wooden supports.

Notched corner strips allow shelf supports—and the shelves that rest on them—to be shifted easily to different levels.

Installing Adjustable Shelves

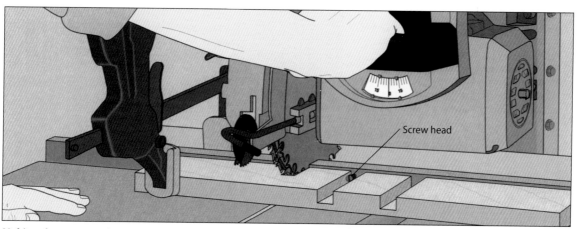

Screw head

Making the corner strips

Rip a board to a 4-inch-width and then cut it to length to reach from top to bottom inside the cabinet. Install a dado head on the radial arm saw, setting the blades to a width to accommodate the thickness of the shelf supports *(page 64)*. Starting at the end that will be at the bottom of the cabinet, cut a dado across the board for the lowest shelf. Slide the board along the fence to cut the second dado at the next shelf position. Before making the cut, to make dadoes the same distance apart, drive a screw into the fence with the head of the fastener against the left edge of the first dado. Then cut the second dado and slide the board along until the left edge of this dado is up against the screw head. Cut the remaining dadoes in this fashion *(above)*, then rip the board into four equal strips.

63

Rabbet

Installing the corner strips

Cut a rabbet at the bottom end of each corner strip to allow it to sit on the bottom of the cabinet while fitting around the rail. To mount the strips, bore two screw holes in each of them near the ends. Make the holes on a drill press in a two-step procedure as for ledger strips in the bottom of a cabinet *(page 62)*. Position each strip in a corner of the cabinet, making sure that the dadoes face the interior as shown. Mark the screw holes in the stiles using an awl, then bore a pilot hole for a No. 8 screw at each point. Use a screwdriver to fasten the strip to the cabinet *(left)*.

Inserting the shelf supports

Measure the distance between the front and back stiles on both sides of the cabinet. Cut shelf supports to fit the gaps between matching pairs of dadoes. Make sure that the supports are wide enough to buttress the shelves properly, and test-fit them *(right)* to ensure that they fit snugly in the dadoes.

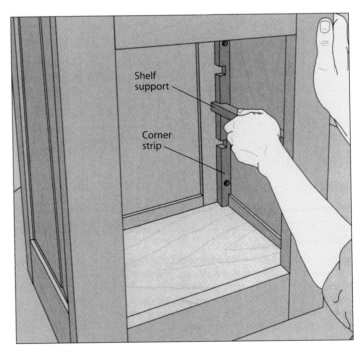

Shelf support

Corner strip

Cutting the shelving to fit

Use plywood or edge-glued boards to make the shelving, cutting each piece to size on a table saw so that the ends will be flush against the cabinet sides and the edges will butt against the stiles. Add edge banding to the visible edge if you are using plywood *(page 41)*. To make a shelf fit, set it on top of the corner strips and outline their shape on the underside of the shelf. Then, secure the shelf in a vise and cut out the corners with a backsaw *(right)*. With edge-glued shelving, you have the option of routing a decorative molding contour along the front edges.

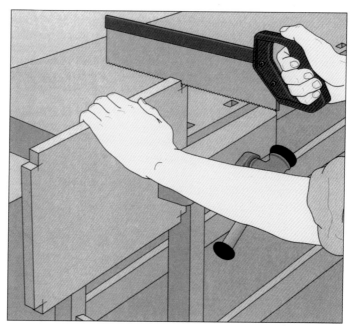

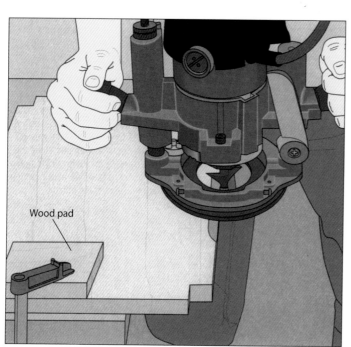

Wood pad

Routing a molding

Place the shelves momentarily inside the cabinet, and mark two lines on the front edge of each one to indicate the beginnings and ends of the moldings. Draw a third line for the desired depth of cut. Protecting the shelf with a wood pad, clamp it to a work surface. Fit a router with an edge-shaping bit, then set the depth of cut. Gripping the router firmly with both hands and resting its base plate on the shelf, turn on the tool. Move the bit pilot up against the edge of the shelf and guide the router against the direction of its bit rotation to cut the molding *(left)*.

Installing a Top

Like the bottom, the top of a frame-and-panel cabinet is made from the same stock as the rest of the piece, usually individual boards edge-glued together. To determine the size, measure the frame and add the width of any molding you plan to install under the lip. Also take into consideration a small amount of overhang at the front and sides. Unless the cabinet will be featured in the middle of a room, make the top panel flush with the back of the case.

Four common methods of attaching tops are illustrated below. One technique features rabbeted blocks, called "buttons," which fit into a groove cut around the top rails. Metal fasteners can be used in the same way. Ledger strips, such as those used to attach a bottom panel to the cabinet, will work equally well for securing a top. Another method calls for the creation of pocket holes in the rails before the case is glued up.

Whatever approach you choose, allow some play in anticipation of wood movement; otherwise, the top will buckle, warp, and force the frame apart. Also, remember to install any drawer-hanging hardware *(page 94)* before putting the top on the cabinet.

Top-fastening options

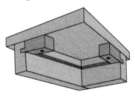

Wood buttons

Metal fasteners

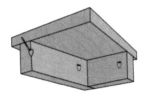

Pocket holes

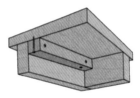

Ledger strips

Wood Buttons to Latch on a Top

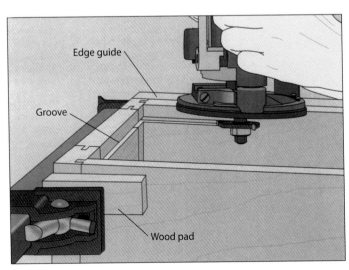

Edge guide

Groove

Wood pad

Cutting a groove in the top rails

Fit a router with a three-wing slotting cutter and set the tool's cutting depth for about ¾ inch. Protecting the surface of the cabinet with wood pads, use bar clamps to hold a guide board flush along the edge on which the router will be riding; this will provide a surface to brace the tool as you cut the groove. For each rail, guide the router along the top edge, moving from left to right *(left)*. Reposition the edge guide before cutting subsequent sides of the cabinet.

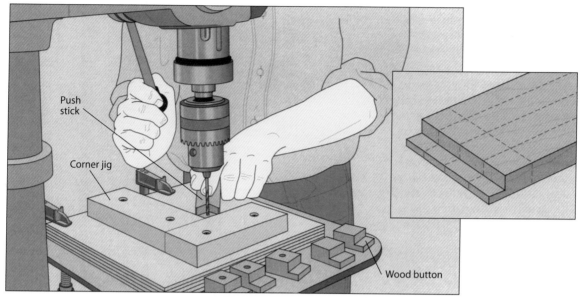

Push
stick

Corner jig

Wood button

Making the buttons

You will need to produce a series of 1-inch-square buttons—at least three for each side and one for about every 6 inches for larger tops. You can mass-produce these pieces from a single board, but choose stock of a thickness equal to the gap between the bottom of the groove cut in step 1 and the top of the rails, less 1⁄16 inch. Cut a 3⁄4-inch rabbet at each end of the board. Then rip the board into 1-inch-wide strips and cut off the buttons about 1¾ inches from the ends *(inset)*. To make holes in the buttons for installation, use a 3⁄16-inch bit and a corner jig fashioned from a scrap of 3⁄4-inch plywood and L-shaped support brackets. Clamp the jig to the drill press table and steady the buttons with a push stick. Bore through the centers of the buttons on the unrabbeted portion *(above)*.

Installing the buttons

Set the cabinet top face down on a work surface, and position the case upside down on top of it. Align the back of the cabinet with the back edge of the top and center the case between its sides. Fit the rabbeted ends of three buttons into the groove in the rail at the back of the cabinet, positioning one in the middle and the other two near the ends. Leave a 1⁄16-inch gap between the lipped ends of the buttons and the bottom of the groove to allow for movement of the wood. Drive screws with a drill to fasten the buttons in place *(left)*.

67

Squaring the top

Install a bar clamp across the front of the case, aligning the bar with the front rail. Using wood pads to focus pressure on the corners, butt one jaw of the clamp on the edge of the top and the other jaw on the front stile. To test for square, measure the gap between the edge of the cabinet and the edge of the top at several points on both sides. The gap should be uniform. If it is not, tighten the clamp *(right)* until the top is correctly positioned on the case. Install the remaining buttons *(page 67)*, at least three per side. The buttons on the sides should be firmly seated in the groove; the buttons on the front—like those on the back—should be backed off slightly from the bottom of the groove.

Wood pad

Pocket Holes

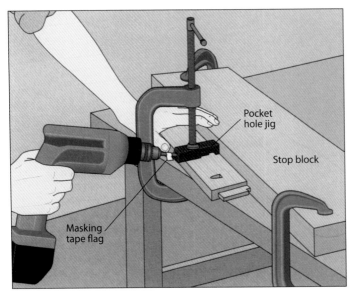

Pocket hole jig

Stop block

Masking tape flag

Boring holes with a commercial jig

Use a drill to bore holes in two steps with two different brad-point bits: one slightly larger than the diameter of the screw heads, so they can be recessed, and one a little larger than the screw shanks to allow a little movement. Clamp a stop block to a work surface, then fit the first bit on the drill. Wrap a strip of masking tape around the bit to mark the drilling depth. Butt the top edge of an upper rail for the cabinet against the stop block, inside surface up, and clamp a commercial pocket hole jig close to one end. Holding the rail firmly, bore the hole, stopping when the strip of tape touches the jig. Reposition the jig to bore another hole in the middle *(left)* and a third one near the other end. Fit the second bit on the drill and bore the clearance holes in the same manner.

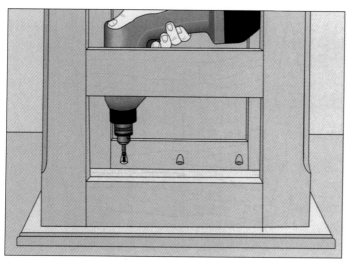

Attaching the top

Once the cabinet has been glued up *(page 61)*, set the top face down on a work surface, and position the case upside down on it as you would when installing wood buttons *(page 67)*. Fit a drill with a screwdriver bit and drive screws to attach the back rail of the cabinet to the top *(left)*. Square the cabinet top the same way you would when installing wood buttons *(page 68)*, then drive screws through the remaining rails.

Securing a Top with Ledger Strips

Installing the wood strips

Cut four ledger strips and bore two sets of holes in them for mounting *(page 62)*. To install the top, first screw the strips in place flush with the top edges of the upper rails of the cabinet *(right)*. Then, set the top panel face down on a work surface and place the cabinet in position on top of it. Screw the top to the strip attached to the back rail and square the top *(page 68)*. Run screws through the remaining ledger strips.

Ledger strip

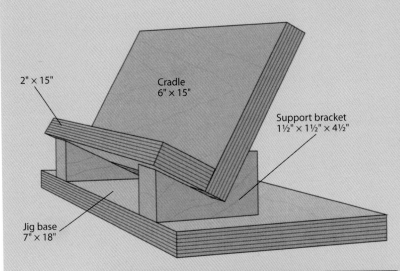

2" × 15"

Cradle
6" × 15"

Support bracket
1½" × 1½" × 4½"

Jig base
7" × 18"

A Pocket Hole Jig

Use a pocket hole jig, shop-built from ¾-inch plywood, to bore pocket holes on a drill press. Refer to the illustration at left for suggested dimensions. For the jig, screw together the two sides of the cradle to form an L. Cut a 90° wedge from each support bracket so that the wide side of the cradle is angled about 15° from the vertical when it sits in the brackets. Screw the brackets to the jig base and glue the cradle to the brackets.

To use the jig, seat the pieces to be drilled in the cradle with their inside surfaces facing out and their top edges in the V of the cradle. Bore the holes in two steps with two different bits as described on page 68. In this case, use a Forstner bit and a brad-point bit.

With the brad-point bit in the chuck, position the jig on the drill press table so that the bit will exit in the center of the top edge of the rail. Clamp the jig to the table and install the Forstner bit in the chuck.

Holding the workpiece firmly in the jig, feed the bit slowly to bore three holes into the rail just deep enough to recess the screw heads. Then, install the brad-point bit in the chuck and bore through the workpiece to complete the pocket holes (left, bottom).

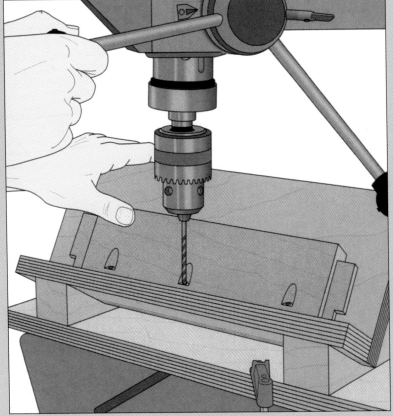

Installing Molding

Whether it is store-bought or shop-made, molding fulfills a key role for the cabinetmaker. On a frame-and-panel cabinet, its principal function is to hide the joint between the top and the rails, creating the illusion of a seamless connection. But molding also gives a piece of furniture a decorative and distinctive look.

By shaping the edges of a piece of hardwood with a router or—as shown below and on the following pages—with a table saw, you can transform some of the same stock used for the cabinet into attractive moldings. Crown, cove, bead, and ogee curve are just a few of the common profiles used in cabinet construction.

When cutting the moldings, make the final pass a very shallow one at half the speed of previous passes. Such a finishing touch should produce a smooth finish that will require only minimal sanding.

The molding for this frame-and-panel cabinet was cut on a table saw equipped with a set of ogee knives.

Preparing and Installing Molding

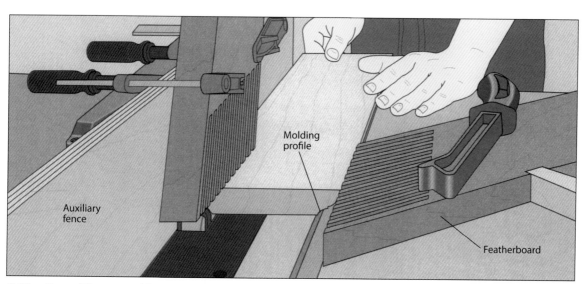

Molding profile

Auxiliary fence

Featherboard

Cutting the molding on a table saw

Select a board long enough to yield moldings for two sides and the front of the cabinet. After fitting out a molding head with the appropriate cutters, screw an auxiliary fence to the metal rip fence. With the metal fence clear of the molding head, position the auxiliary fence over the table opening and turn on the saw. Crank up the head to cut a notch in the wood. To secure the workpiece, clamp featherboards to the fence above the molding head and to the saw table bearing against the edge of the stock. Then, raise the cutters ⅛ inch above the table and feed the workpiece into the molding head. Finish the pass with a push stick. For a deeper cut, make additional passes, raising the cutters ⅛ inch at a time. Repeat the procedure to shape the opposite edge of the workpiece *(above)*. Install a combination blade on the saw, then rip the molding from the edges of the stock. Cut the molding to length for one side of the cabinet, making a 45° miter at one end of the piece.

71

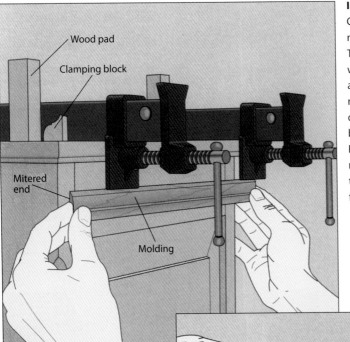

Wood pad

Clamping block

Mitered end

Molding

Installing the molding on one side

Cut four wood pads and two short pieces of molding to serve as special clamping blocks. Turned upside down, the blocks will mesh with the molding being glued in place. Apply an even layer of adhesive to the back of the molding, being careful not to slop any glue on the top edge. The decorative trim should bond to the rails, not to the top of the cabinet. Position the molding on the side rail *(left)*, making sure that it butts against the cabinet top and that its mitered end is flush with the front stile.

Tightening the clamps

Protecting the opposite side of the cabinet with wood pads, install two clamps across the top of the case. To hold the molding firmly, place the clamping block between the molding and the wood pads. Tighten each clamp a little at time *(right)* until a thin bead of glue squeezes out of the joint. Remove any excess adhesive.

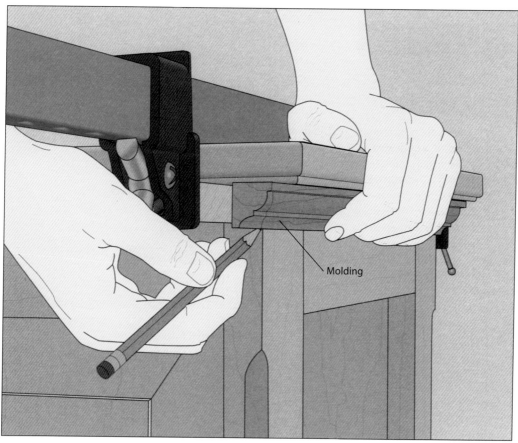

Molding

Installing molding on the cabinet front

With the piece of side molding still clamped to the cabinet, measure the width of the front of the case. Cut a piece of molding slightly longer than this width, making a 45° miter cut at the end that will butt against the molding already in place. Hold the new piece in place and use a pencil to mark a cutting line on the unmitered end *(above)*, angling out from the corner.

Cut the piece of molding to length, making a 45° miter in line with your cutting mark. Once the glue for the side piece has dried, remove the clamps and install the piece of front molding *(page 72)*. Repeat the process to cut and install the remaining piece of molding.

Shop Tip

An alternative method for clamping on moldings

To simplify the clamping operation, make two triangular wood pads, which will enable you to use C clamps to hold the molding in place. Glue a strip of sandpaper to the edge of each pad to prevent it from slipping when clamping pressure is applied.

Drawers

In essence, a drawer is nothing more than a box without a top—a front, a back, two sides and a bottom. Individual examples, however, belie this simplicity. They run the gamut from the modern kitchen drawer slamming shut on metal slides to the drawer of a well-made Victorian desk whispering home with a nearly airtight sigh. The former is often an anonymous, interchangeable unit with a false front. The latter may be a finicky individual precisely fit to an opening in a particular piece of furniture, its unique face blending beautifully with the grain of the wood surrounding it.

Pulled open, a drawer reveals more of its personality. Each of its five pieces may be cut from a different wood. The front, which shows most, is chosen for its species, color and grain; the thinner sides for long wear; the back for strength; the bottom for stability.

Not only is the front the most visible part of a drawer, it also takes the most abuse. As you will discover in the joinery section of this chapter *(page 78)*, keeping it attached to the sides requires a durable, solid joint.

A drawer's most basic function is to hold things. But it must also slip in and out of the piece of furniture housing it without jamming or chattering. As with joinery, mounting a drawer offers many choices *(page 89)*. Every method must support the drawer, prevent it from tipping as it is pulled out and stop it as it slides home. The perfect drawer will glide nearly out, then hesitate a bit; drawer stops *(page 97)* prevent the unit from being inadvertently pulled all the way out or pushed too far in.

Different types of furniture demand different methods of mounting drawers. In carcases, drawers can be side-mounted: grooves routed in their sides slide on thin strips of wood attached directly to the cabinet sides. They can also be supported by a U-shaped frame with runners at the sides and a rail at the front. Here, the drawer slides on the bottom edges of its sides—a traditional technique called bottom-run. In frame-and-panel cases, drawer supports sit on strips attached to the frames only.

Commercial metal drawer slide runners—like those found on file drawers—provide a wheeled side-mounting option. One-half of the hardware attaches to the carcase and the other half to the drawer sides. Used extensively in kitchen cabinetwork, metal slides can support great weight and provide access to the very back of the drawer.

Whether meant to hold pajamas in a quickly made child's chest or nightgowns in an heirloom highboy, drawers will form an integral part of many of your cabinet construction projects. Each of the thousands of times someone opens one of these drawers, he or she will be reminded of the care you took to build them.

Sized to fit between grooves cut in the sides of a drawer, a plywood bottom panel slides into position. The panel will bottom out in a groove in the front and be nailed to the back to secure it in place.

Set off by the simplicity of a metallic single-pull handle, a solid wood drawer glides smoothly in and out of a frame-and-panel cabinet. Grooves routed into the drawer sides run along supports attached to the frame of the cabinet.

Anatomy of a Drawer

Drawer-making consists of three distinct steps: joining boards together to form a box, mounting the drawer in a piece of furniture and installing hardware. Each step must be performed precisely if a drawer is to combine grace and strength, gliding smoothly in a piece of furniture while being sturdy enough to bear the weight of its contents.

Although virtually all drawers share the basic features of the one shown below *(center)*, there are an array of variations. Before making your first cut, consider the options for each step. For example, from among the joints illustrated at right, there is one to satisfy virtually any requirement. Each joint has different characteristics in terms of strength and durability, level of difficulty, and

appearance and suitability for different types of stock and furniture. You can allow personal preference to guide your selection, but make sure you choose a strong joint to attach the drawer front to the sides. This is the part of the drawer that endures the most stress.

The success of the drawer-mounting operation hinges on how well the drawer has been put together. Three different methods for mounting a drawer in a carcase are shown in this chapter *(below, left)* as well as one technique suitable for frame-and-panel cabinets. Although each method permits some adjustment, a drawer out-of-square by a wide margin will be almost impossible to install.

Drawer Fronts

False front: A separate front is nailed over the structural front; conceals end grain of drawer sides.

Lipped front: A rabbeted front creates a lip that serves as an overhang; useful for concealing commercial runners when the drawer is closed; lip performs double duty as drawer stop.

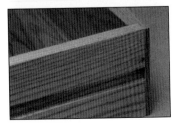

Flush front: Allows the drawer to fit entirely within the cabinet; also known as an inset drawer.

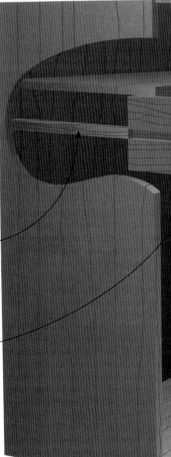

Drawer slide
Sits in groove routed in drawer side; screwed to carcase side panel.

Bottom panel
Typically ¼- inch plywood; fits in groove routed in drawer sides and front.

Drawer Joints

Rabbet
For back-to-side joints on most drawers; also strong enough for joining the front to the sides if reinforced with screws or nails; suitable for solid wood or plywood.

Through dovetail
Strong, decorative joint for any drawer corner; end grain of drawer sides can be concealed with false front; appropriate for solid wood but not plywood.

Half-blind dovetail
The traditional joint for connecting the front to the sides; conceals end grain of sides; suitable only for solid wood.

Dado
Can be used to join the front to the sides and the back to the sides; for solid wood or plywood.

Double dado
For any corner of small, light-duty drawer; conceals end grain of sides and front; suitable only for solid wood.

Drawer-Mounting Methods

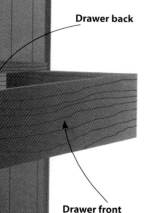

Drawer back

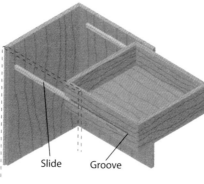

Slide   Groove

Side-mounted
Wooden slides screwed to carcase side panels run in grooves routed in drawer sides.

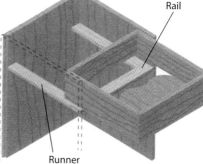

Rail

Runner

Drawer front
Typically thicker than sides, back and bottom; may be covered by a false front.

Bottom-run
Drawer slides on rail and runner assembly. Twin tenons at ends of rail are glued into double mortises cut into carcase panels; one edge of runners is rabbeted and fits into groove cut into panels.

Drawer side
Joined to front and back with any of a variety of joints; groove shown meshes with drawer slide.

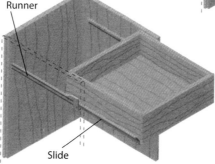

Runner

Slide

Commercial slide runners
Metal slides screwed to drawer sides mesh with runners screwed to carcase.

Drawer Joinery

The first step in drawer-making is to think the process through from beginning to end. The various stages of the operation are related; the finished dimensions of a drawer front, for example, can depend on the joinery method you choose. And drawer hanging methods can influence the way a drawer is built.

Once you have settled on the size of drawer, choose a joinery method *(page 77)*, a method of hanging, and the style of front you will use; then size your stock. Cut the front, back and sides to fit the opening, choosing the most visually appealing piece for the front. The grain of the drawer should run horizontally when it is installed. Make sure that the best side of each piece faces outward; mark it with an X as a reminder.

Not all the parts of a drawer undergo the same stresses. The front takes the hardest beating, the sides a little less, the back less still. Cabinetmakers take this into account when they build drawers. Many will plane the parts differently depending on how sturdy they need to be. Thus, the front can be thicker than the sides and the sides thicker than the back.

Woodworkers often use different joints at different corners. The choice depends not merely on the desired visual effect, but also on the stresses the joint will face. A joint that might be adequate to connect the sides to the back of a drawer may not be strong enough to join the front to the sides.

The following pages present an assortment of joinery methods. Some are suitable for front-to-side joints, others

are strictly for back-to-side joints, while still others can be used at any corner. You also need to keep in mind the type of wood you are using. Some joints, such as the dovetail and the double dado, can be used only with solid wood, while others—the rabbet and the dado, for example—work equally well with plywood or solid wood.

For the strongest and most attractive joint, choose the through dovetail, which can be cut quickly and accurately using a jig *(page 82)*. You can also saw one by hand as you would to join carcase sides *(page 29)*. Unless you will be installing a false front *(page 99)*, a half-blind dovetail *(page 84)* may be a better choice. Also called the lapped dovetail, the half-blind dovetail conceals the end grain of the sides.

Rabbet and lipped rabbet joints *(page 79)* are easy to cut and are strong enough to use at any corner of a drawer, particularly if reinforced with screws or nails. The main difference between the two joints is that the drawer front in a lipped rabbet joint overhangs the sides. As a result, the front must be cut larger than the opening.

Simple to construct, the dado and double dado joints *(page 80)* are ideal choices for small, light-duty drawers. The double dado conceals end grain, making it a visually appealing alternative to the dado.

Like other operations in cabinet construction, drawer-building demands accuracy and patience. Make test joints to fine-tune your tools and measurements before cutting into stock, and periodically test-fit a drawer to ensure it will fit its opening perfectly.

Different joints for different purposes: A simple dado joint is sufficient to join the back to the sides of a drawer. But the front requires a stronger joint—in this case, a double dado, also known as a concealed dado-and-tongue.

Rabbet Joints

Using a dado head on the table saw
On your table saw install a dado head slightly wider than the thickness of the drawer sides and crank it below the table. Attach an auxiliary fence and set the width of cut equal to the thickness of the sides. Turn on the saw and raise the blades to notch the auxiliary fence. Set the cutting height to no more than one-half the thickness of the drawer front. To cut the rabbets, butt the edge of the front against the fence. Holding the workpiece flush against the miter gauge, feed it face down into the dado head. Flip the board around and repeat the cut at the opposite end *(right)*.

Auxiliary fence

Drawer front

Lipped Rabbet Joints

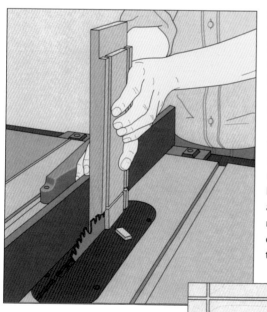

Cutting a lip in a drawer front
To cut lipped rabbets around the edges of a drawer front, mark lines on its inside face to allow for an overhang of at least ⅜ inch. Also mark the rabbet depth on its edges—up to one-half the thickness of the drawer front. Cut the rabbets in two steps, first notching the inside face of the front, then feeding the stock into the blade on end and on edge. To make the first cuts, set the blade height to the depth of the rabbet. Then feed the stock inside face down into the blade to cut along the marked lines *(inset)*. To make the remaining cuts, set the blade height to the width of the rabbets. Align the blade with the marks for the rabbet depth, then butt the fence against the stock. Keeping the drawer front flush against the fence, feed it on end into the blade to complete one rabbet. Turn the board over and repeat to cut the rabbet at the other end *(left)*. Then feed the stock into the blade on edge to cut the rabbets on the top and bottom edges.

Inside face of drawer front

Dado Joints

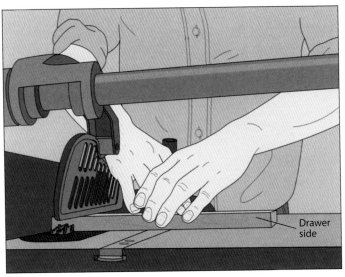

Cutting dadoes in drawer sides

A dado cut about ½ inch from the back end of each side serves as an effective back-to-side joint. On your table saw install a dado head the same width as the drawer back. Position the rip fence about ½ inch from the blades and set the cutting height no higher than one-half the stock thickness. Butt the drawer side against the fence. Then, holding the board firmly against the miter gauge, make the cut.

Drawer side

Double Dado Joints

Cutting dadoes in a drawer front

Mark one end of the board to divide its thickness into thirds. Then, on your table saw attach a dado head whose width equals one-third the thickness of the drawer front. Next, install a commercial tenoning jig; the model shown slides in the miter slot. Protecting the stock with a wood pad, clamp the drawer front to the jig. Move the jig sideways to align the marks on the stock with the dado head to cut out the dado in the middle third of the board. Slide the jig along to feed the stock into the blades. Turn the drawer front over and clamp it to the jig to cut the dado at the other end *(right)*.

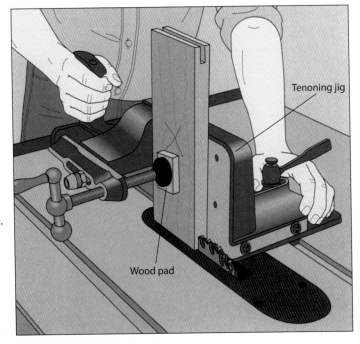

Tenoning jig

Wood pad

Trimming the dado tongues
Install an auxiliary fence, then mark a cutting line on the edge of the drawer front to divide one of the tongues on its inside face in half. With the stock flush against the miter gauge, inside face down, align the marked line with the dado head. Butt the fence against the stock. Notch the fence *(page 79)*, then set the cutting height to trim the half-tongue. Holding the drawer front firmly against the gauge, feed it into the dado head. Turn the board around and repeat the procedure at the other end *(right)*.

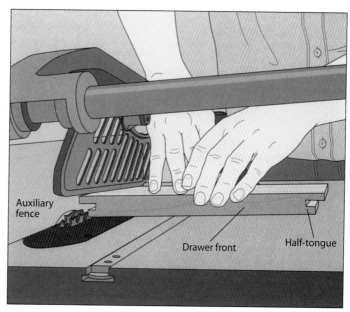

Auxiliary fence

Drawer front

Half-tongue

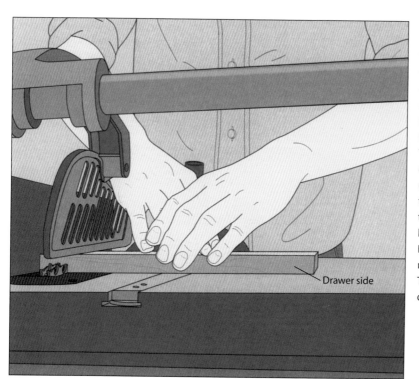

Drawer side

Cutting matching dadoes in the drawer sides
To join the drawer sides to the front, cut a dado near the front end of each side. The dadoes need to mesh with the half-tongues on the front. First, set the cutting height to the length of the half-tongues. To set the width of cut, butt the drawer side against the front and use a pencil to outline the half-tongue on the drawer side. Align the marks with the dado head, then butt the rip fence against the stock. Holding the board flush against the miter gauge, feed it into the blades. Then repeat the cut on the other drawer side.

Drawers

Back to **Basics**

81

Through Dovetail Joints

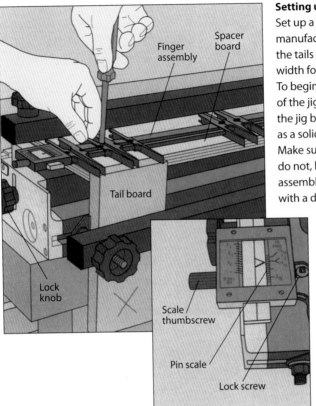

Finger assembly

Spacer board

Tail board

Lock knob

Scale thumbscrew

Pin scale

Lock screw

Setting up the router jig

Set up a router jig for cutting dovetails following the manufacturer's instructions. For the model shown, adjusting the tails on a finger assembly automatically sets the proper width for the pins on the opposite side of the same assembly. To begin, cut a piece of ¾-inch plywood to fit across the top of the jig as a spacer board, then clamp the board between the jig body and the finger assembly. The spacer board serves as a solid base for the assembly and helps reduce tear-out. Make sure that the assembly lock screws face up; if they do not, loosen the scale thumbscrews, remove the finger assembly from its support arms and flip it over. Fit a router with a dovetail bit, then set the pin scale on both ends of the finger assembly to the bit diameter *(inset)*. Tighten the thumbscrews. Clamp the tail board (one of the drawer's sides) to the jig, outside-face out. Loosen the lock knobs on each side of the jig, then slightly raise the finger assembly and tighten the knobs. Lay out the fingers across the end of the tail board to set the size and spacing of the tails. Leave a few fingers on each side of the tail board to keep the router steady when it is cutting. There should be one finger at each edge of the board to make half-tails. Once you are satisfied with the spacing— symmetrical or asymmetrical, depending on your preference—tighten the lock screws *(left)*.

Cutting the tails

With the tail board still clamped to the jig, loosen the scale thumbscrews. Turn over the finger assembly and slide it along the support arms until both scales indicate the ALL position. Loosen the lock knobs on the side of the jig, lower the finger assembly on the spacer board and tighten the knobs, making sure the assembly is sitting squarely on the spacer board. Use a pin board as a guide to scribe a line across the tail board marking the cutting depth. Then, position the router on the jig, its base plate resting on the finger assembly, and set the tip of the bit ¹⁄₁₆ inch below the marked line. Turn on the router and cut out the waste between the tails *(right)*. Rout from right to left, keeping the tool flat against the finger assembly. Turn the board over, secure it to the jig and cut the tails at the other end the same way. Follow the same procedure to cut the tails of the other drawer side.

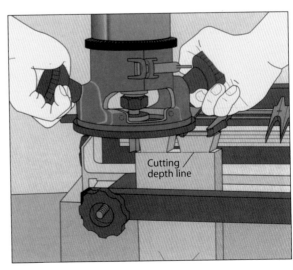

Cutting depth line

Cutting the pins

Remove the tail board and turn over the finger assembly. Set the pin scale to the diameter of the dovetail bit. Then fit the router with a straight-cutting bit and clamp the pin board—the drawer front—to the jig, outside-face out. Use a tail board butted against the pin board to mark a line for the cutting depth. Place the router on the jig and set the tip of the bit 1/16 inch below the marked line. Cut out the waste between the pins the same way you routed out the tails *(left)*. Then, remove the pin board and test-fit the joint. If the fit is too tight, loosen the scale thumbscrews and slide the finger assembly about 1/8 inch toward the back of the jig. Tighten the thumbscrews *(below)*. Make another pass with the router to remove more waste between the fingers. Test-fit the joint again, and make any necessary adjustments. Once you are satisfied with the fit, turn the board over, secure it to the jig and cut the pins at the other end. Cut the pins at both ends of the drawer back the same way.

Cutting depth line

Half-Blind Dovetail Joints

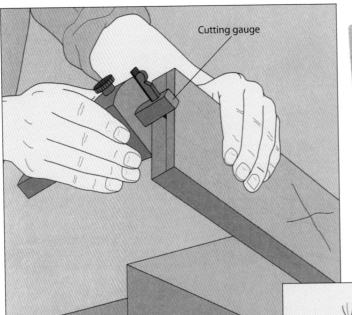

Cutting gauge

The half-blind dovetail makes an ideal joint for building drawers: The tails on the side piece are visible but their end grain is concealed by the drawer front. The joint can be cut by hand, as shown in the following pages, or by a router in combination with a template or a jig.

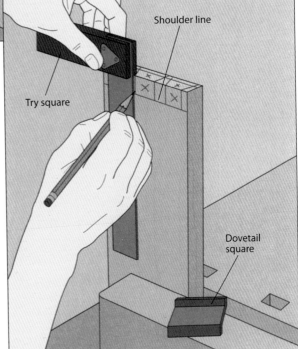

Shoulder line

Try square

Dovetail square

Marking the pin board

Mark the outside faces of the boards with an X. Then set a cutting gauge to about two-thirds the thickness of the pin board and mark a line across the end, closer to the outside than the inside face *(above)*. Adjust the cutting gauge to the thickness of the stock and scribe a line around the ends of the pin boards to mark the shoulder line of the tails. Next, use a dovetail square to outline the pins on an end of the pin board; the wide part of the pins should be on the inside face of the stock. There are no strict guidelines for spacing dovetail pins, but for most drawers, starting with a half-pin at each edge and adding two evenly spaced pins in between makes for a strong and attractive joint. To complete the marking, secure the pin board in a vise and use a try square and a pencil to extend the lines on the board end to the shoulder line on its inside face *(right)*. Mark the waste sections with an X as you go.

Cutting the pins

Secure one pin board in a vise with the outside face of the stock toward you, then cut along the edges of the pins with a dovetail saw, working your way from one board edge to the other. (Some woodworkers prefer to cut all the left-hand edges of the pins first, then all the right-hand edges.) Hold the board steady and align the saw blade just to the waste side of the cutting line; angle the saw toward the waste to avoid cutting into the pins. Use smooth, even strokes, allowing the saw to cut on the push stroke. Continue the cut just to the shoulder line, then repeat to cut the pins at the other end of the board.

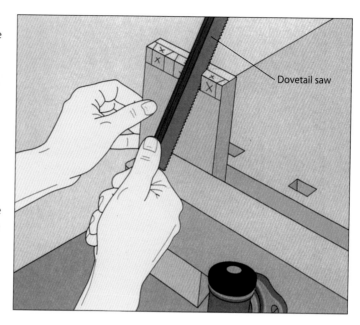

Dovetail saw

Removing the bulk of the waste

Set the panel inside-face up on a work surface and clamp a guide block to it, aligning its edge with the waste side of the shoulder line. Starting at one edge of the stock, hold the flat side of a chisel about 1/16 inch from the guide block; the tool should be no wider than the narrowest part of the waste section. With the chisel square to the face of the board, use a wooden mallet to strike it, scoring a line about 1/8-inch-deep into the waste section. Then hold the chisel flat side down and square to the end of the board about 1/8 inch below the top surface. Strike the chisel to remove a thin layer of waste. Continue until you reach the scribed line on the end of the board, then pare away any excess. Repeat the process with the remaining waste sections.

Guide block

Final paring

Working on one waste section at a time, press the flat side of the chisel against the walls of the section with the thumb of your left hand; with your right hand, push the chisel toward the shoulder line, shaving away the last slivers of waste *(left)*. If necessary, tap the chisel gently with a wooden mallet.

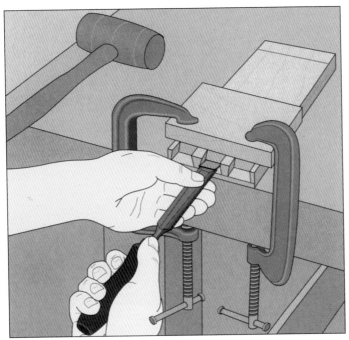

Marking and cutting the tails

Set a tail board inside-face up on a work surface. Hold one of the pin boards end-down with its inside face aligned with the shoulder line of the tail board. Use a pencil to outline the tails on the tail board *(right)*, then extend the lines on the board end using a try square. Mark the waste with Xs, then outline the tails on the other end of the board the same way. Remove the waste as you would when cutting dovetail joints for carcase panels *(page 31)*. Repeat the procedure for the other tail board.

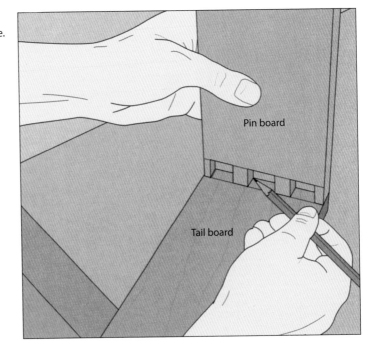

Pin board

Tail board

Assembling a Drawer

Drawer Assembly

Preparing the drawer for a bottom panel

Dry-fit the parts of the drawer, then clamp the unit securely, aligning the bars of the clamps with the drawer sides. Use a pencil to identify the parts that fit together to make reassembly easier later when you glue up. To install a bottom panel, rout a groove along the inside of the drawer. First, mark a line ½ inch from the bottom edge of the front, back and sides. Then, fit a router with a ¼-inch three-wing slotting cutter and mount the tool in a router table. Set the drawer right-side up on the table and align the cutter with the marked line. Starting at the middle of one drawer side, feed the stock into the cutter. Keeping the pilot bearing butted against the workpiece, feed the drawer clockwise *(right)*. Continue pivoting the drawer on the table until you return to your starting point.

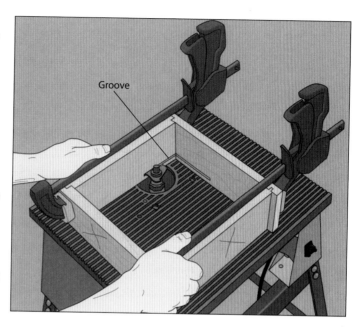

Groove

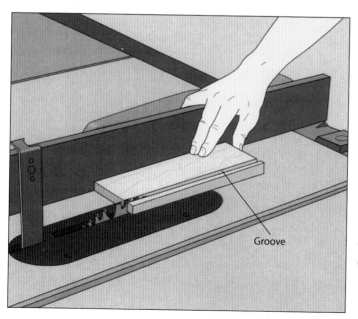

Groove

Making the bottom panel and preparing the back

For the bottom panel, cut a piece of ¼-inch plywood to fit the opening, adding the depth of the grooves to its width and the depth of one groove and the thickness of the back to its length. Next, remove the clamps and trim the bottom of the drawer back with a table saw to allow you to slide the bottom panel into position. With the back inside face up on the saw table, align the top edge of the groove you cut before with the blade. Butt the rip fence against the stock, then feed the back into the blade to make the cut, straddling the fence with the fingers of your right hand. **(Caution: Blade guard removed for clarity.)**

Drawers

*Back to **Basics***

87

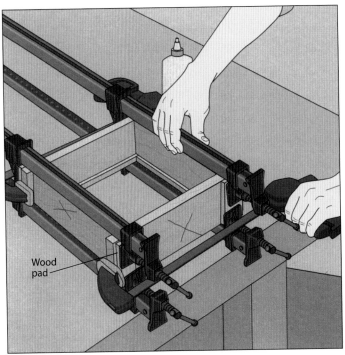

Wood
pad

Gluing up the drawer

Before gluing up the drawer, decide how you will mount it *(page 89)*, since some methods require you to prepare the drawer sides before final assembly. Then, sand the surfaces that will be difficult to access after glue-up. Squeeze some glue on the contacting surfaces of the joints and spread the adhesive evenly with a brush. Assemble the drawer, then arrange two bar clamps on a work surface and lay the drawer on them, aligning the drawer sides with the bars of the clamps. Install two more clamps along the top of the drawer and two more across the back and front. Place a wood pad between the stock and the clamp jaws to avoid marring the wood. (Do not place a pad on a lipped drawer front, as it will prevent the joints from closing.) Tighten the clamps just enough to fully close the joints *(left)*, then use a try square to check whether the corners are at right angles. If they are not, use a bar clamp placed diagonally to correct the problem *(page 61)*. Finish tightening the clamps until a bead of glue squeezes out of the joints, checking as you go that the corners are square. Once the adhesive has dried, remove any dried glue with a paint scraper. Slide the bottom panel into place, then drive a few finishing nails through it and into the bottom edge of the drawer back to fix it in position.

Shop Tip

Fixing a loose drawer bottom

If a drawer bottom is loose, use shop-made wedges to tighten the fit. Begin by using a table saw to rip a few thin strips of wood from a board, angling the blade to produce one narrow edge. Then, cut the strips into smaller pieces. Set the drawer upside down on a work surface and install a wedge into any gap between the bottom panel and the sides or front of the drawer. Coat the strips with glue, then insert the tapered end into the gap; use a hammer to tap them snugly into place. Once the glue has dried, use a wood chisel to sever any part of the wedges protruding from the grooves.

Mounting a Drawer

There are probably as many drawer-mounting methods as there are drawer joints. The technique you select is determined by the piece of furniture in which the drawer will be housed: a frame-and-panel cabinet requires different hanging methods than does a carcase. The following pages consider both types of casework.

A drawer can be supported in one of two ways: along its sides or along its bottom. As shown at right and on page 90, a side-mounted drawer has grooves routed in its sides before glue up, allowing it to run along slides attached to the carcase. A side-mounted drawer in a frame-and-panel case *(page 94)* is held in place by the same system of corner strips and supports used to install shelves.

Commercial slide runners *(page 95)* offer another method for side-mounting drawers in a carcase. Although many purists regard them as a poor alternative, commercial runners are actually stronger than wood runners, making them ideal for drawers that will bear heavy loads.

A popular way to support a bottom-run drawer is by a system of runners and rails affixed to a carcase, as shown on pages 92 and 93.

A side-mounted drawer is slid into a carcase for test-fitting. A lipped front conceals the runners and grooves when the drawer is closed.

Some woodworkers prefer to rout a groove in the carcase sides and install a shelf, which serves not only as a drawer support but as a dust panel as well.

Side-Mounting: Carcase

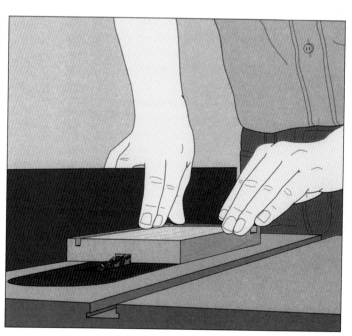

Cutting grooves in the drawer sides
Before final assembly, cut a groove in the outside face of each drawer side. There are no rigid guidelines for the groove width, but it should be able to accommodate slides that are large enough to support the drawer. On your table saw install a dado head the same width as the groove. Draw cutting lines for the groove width in the middle of the leading end of one drawer side; also mark the depth of the groove—no more than one-half the stock thickness. Butt the lines for the groove width against the dado head, then crank the blades up to the depth line; position the rip fence flush against the stock and make the cut. If the groove width exceeds the width of the dado head, turn the board end for end and make another pass. Repeat to cut the groove in the other drawer side.

Ripping the drawer slides

Install a combination blade on your table saw. Crosscut a board so that its length is a few inches shorter than the width of the carcase side panels. Then position the rip fence to set a cutting width equal to the width of the grooves you cut in the drawer sides, less $\frac{1}{32}$ inch for clearance. Cut two slides from the edge of the board, using a push stick to feed the stock into the blade *(right)*. Smooth one edge of the slides with a hand plane to make sure that they will rest flush against the side panels of the carcase. **(Caution: Blade guard removed for clarity.)**

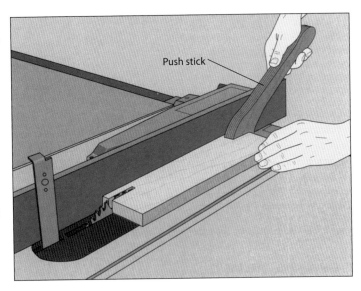

Push stick

Installing the slides

Insert the drawer into the carcase and hold it in place while using a pencil to mark the location of the grooves on the front edges of the side panels. Then use a carpenter's square to extend the marks across the inside faces of the panels. To mount the slides, bore three holes for countersinking screws; make the clearance holes slightly wider than the screw shanks to allow for wood movement. Holding the slides back from the front edge of the carcase between the marked lines on the side panels, screw them in place *(left)*. Test-fit the drawer. If it is too loose, add shims under the slides; if it is too tight, enlarge the groove in the drawer side. You can also recess the slides in the carcase sides using a jig *(page 91)*.

Dado-routing jig for drawer supports

To rout a series of evenly spaced dadoes in the side panels of a carcase for drawer runners, use the shop-made jig shown at right. Dimensions depend on the size of the carcase and the spacing between the runners.

For the jig, cut a piece of ¼-inch plywood as a base. Make it about the same width as the carcase side panels and a few inches longer than the gap between the runners. Set the jig base on a work surface and place a router on it near one end. Mark the screw holes in the router base plate on the jig base; also draw a spot directly below the tool's chuck. Bore holes for the screws; cut a hole below the chuck wide enough to allow clearance for the router bit. Screw the jig base to the machine's base plate and install a straight-cutting bit the same width as the dadoes you wish to rout.

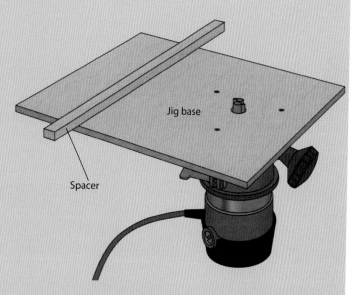

Jig base

Spacer

Side panel

Next, cut a spacer to fit snugly in the dadoes; make it slightly longer than the width of the panels. Screw the spacer to the bottom of the jig base, making the distance between it and the router bit equal to the spacing you want between the runners.

To use the jig, clamp a side panel inside-face up to the work surface. Set the jig on the panel with the spacer flush against one end of the workpiece and the router bit at one edge. Gripping the router firmly, turn it on and feed the tool across the panel to rout the dado; keep the spacer flush against the panel. Turn off the router, then insert the spacer in the dado, repositioning the clamps, as necessary. Rout the next dado, sliding the spacer in the first dado. Continue until all the dadoes have been cut, then repeat the operation on the other side panel.

Bottom-Run: Carcase

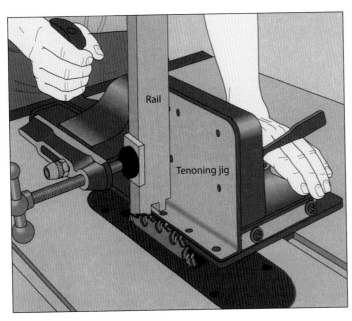

Rail

Tenoning jig

Preparing the rail

Crosscut a board long enough to span the gap between the side panels, adding the thickness of one panel to allow for twin tenons at the ends of the rail. For the twin tenons, mark the ends of the stock to divide its width into fifths. Then, install a dado head wide enough to cut out the waste between two of the marks. Set the cutting height at one-half the thickness of the panels. Next, install a commercial tenoning jig on your saw table. Clamp the rail to the jig end up; shift the device sideways to align the marks on the rail with the dado head to cut the shoulder in the middle fifth of the board. To make the cut, push the jig forward, feeding the stock into the blades. Move the jig to cut the shoulders at the outside edge of the rail. Turn the stock around to cut the remaining shoulder *(left)*. Then cut the twin tenons at the other end.

Chiseling the double mortises

Hold the end of the rail against each carcase side panel at the desired height of the drawer bottom and outline the mortises. Extend the lines to the edge of the panels, then butt the two workpieces face to face to make sure the marks are at the same height. To cut the mortises, first clamp a panel to a work surface. Then, starting at an end of one outline, hold a mortising chisel square to the face of the panel and strike the handle with a wooden mallet. Use a chisel the same width as the mortise and be sure that the beveled side is facing the waste. Make another cut ⅛ inch from the first. Continue until you reach the other end of the outline, using the chisel to lever out the waste to the required depth. Chop out the adjacent mortise and the double mortise on the other panel the same way. Test-fit the twin tenons; widen or deepen a mortise with the chisel, as required.

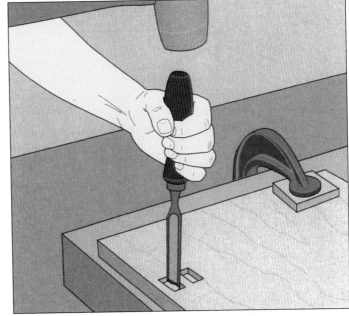

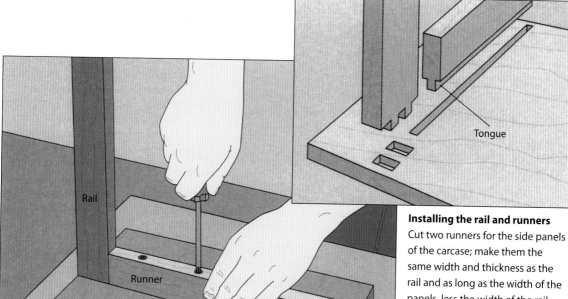

Rail

Runner

Tongue

Installing the rail and runners

Cut two runners for the side panels of the carcase; make them the same width and thickness as the rail and as long as the width of the panels, less the width of the rail. Cut a tongue in the middle of one edge of the runners about one-third the width and thickness of the runner. Rout a matching groove in the carcase side panels; center the slot on the double mortise for the twin tenons *(inset)*. To mount the runners, first bore a series of holes for countersinking screws; the clearance holes should allow for wood movement. Then, fit the rail into the double mortise in one side panel and slot the runner into the panel. Making sure that the runner is butted squarely against the rail, screw it in place. Repeat to mount the runner to the other carcase side panel. At the same time that you glue up the carcase, spread some adhesive on the rail's twin tenons and the double mortises in the side panels and fit the two together. The clamping setup for the carcase will hold the rail in place while the glue dries.

Shop Tip

Fixing a bowed drawer side

A bowed side can prevent a drawer from sliding properly; a shop-made glue block will correct the problem. Cut the block slightly narrower than the gap between the bottom panel and the bottom edge of the drawer side. Spread some glue on the surfaces of the block that contact the drawer, then butt the piece of wood against the bottom panel and drawer side as shown, centering it between the front and back. Install a clamp across the middle of the drawer, tightening it until the side straightens out. Once the glue has dried, remove the clamp.

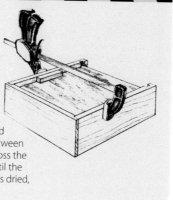

Side-Mounting: Frame-and-Panel

The same system of corner strips and supports for installing adjustable shelves in frame-and-panel cabinets can be used to mount a drawer. Before the corner strips are screwed to the stiles of the cabinet, they are held in place with handscrews. This way, the drawer can be test-fitted in the opening and the strips can be raised or lowered as needed. Once the drawer slides smoothly and is centered, the strips are fixed to the cabinet.

Attaching corner strips and supports

Prepare the drawer sides as you would to side-mount the drawer in a carcase *(page 89)*. Glue up the drawer, then hold it at the desired height in the cabinet and mark the position of its grooves on the stiles. To mount the drawer, use corner strips and supports *(page 63)*. Make the strips long enough to reach from the top edge of the cabinet to the bottom of the drawer. Rout a dado across the strips, aligning it with the marks you made on the stiles. Cut two supports to fit between the dadoes, less $\frac{1}{16}$ inch for clearance. Hold the corner strips flush against the stiles with handscrews, lining up the dadoes with the position marks. Fit the supports in the dadoes, then slide the drawer into position. It should move smoothly and sit centered and level in the opening. If not, loosen the handscrews and adjust the height of the corner strips, as necessary *(right)*. Screw the wood strips to the stiles.

94

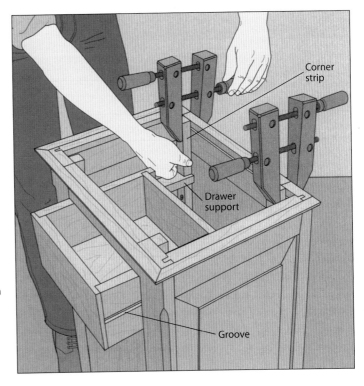

Corner strip

Drawer support

Groove

Commercial Slide Runners: Carcase

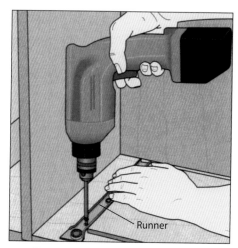

Runner

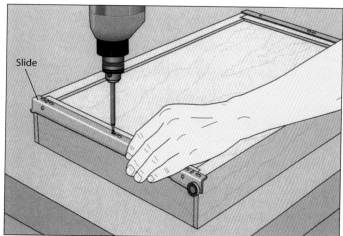

Slide

Installing the runners

Install commercial slide runners following the manufacturer's instructions. The type shown consists of two parts: runners that attach to the carcase and slides that are screwed to the drawer. To help position the runners, cut a piece of ¼-inch plywood to fit between the bottom of the carcase and the bottom edge of the runner. If the drawer is directly under a shelf or the carcase top, trim ½ inch from the plywood jig to allow for clearance during installation, when the drawer must be lifted slightly to fit the wheels into the runners. With the carcase on its side, butt the plywood piece against the bottom of the side panel. Then place the runner against the jig, setting it back from the front edge of the panel to allow for the thickness of the drawer front. Mark the screw holes on the side panel, then bore a pilot hole at each point. Screw the runner to the panel (above). Repeat to fasten a runner to the other side panel.

Installing the slides

Hold the slides on the drawer, then test-fit it in the carcase. If the drawer is loose, shim the runners; if the drawer binds, plane some stock from its sides (page 96). Then set the drawer upside down, position the slides and mark the screw holes on the drawer. Bore pilot holes, then screw the slides in place (above).

Shop Tip

Positioning Jig

To help you correctly position commercial slides on drawer sides, use a shop-made jig. Cut a rabbet in a scrap board; make the depth of the rabbet equal to the desired distance between the slide and the bottom of the drawer side. To use the jig, hold it up against the bottom of the drawer side as shown. Then set the slide on the drawer side, bottom edge butted against the jig. Holding the slide and jig in place, mark the screw holes. Then bore pilot holes and screw the slide to the drawer.

Fine-Tuning Drawer Fit

Planing the drawer sides

A drawer may bind in a piece of furniture even after a thorough sanding. If the top or bottom of the drawer rubs against part of the casework, plane the top. If the sides bind, remove the drawer and mark any shiny areas on the sides—high spots that can be shaved off with a hand plane. To secure the drawer for planing, clamp a wide board to a workbench with one edge extending over the side. Hang the drawer on the board so that the binding side is facing up. Then clamp another board to the workbench, butting it against the drawer; use a bench dog to keep the second board from moving. Gripping the plane with both hands, shave off the marked spots with smooth, even strokes *(right)*. Test-fit the drawer in its opening periodically, planing the sides until the drawer fits perfectly.

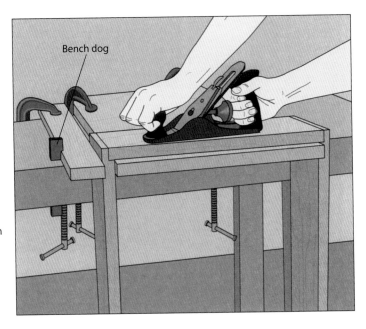

Bench dog

Planing the top of a drawer

To hold the drawer in place, set it on a work surface and nail three scrap boards to the table flush against the sides and back of the drawer. Gripping a hand plane firmly, make a smooth pass on the top edges of the drawer sides from the front of the drawer to the back. Move to the adjacent side of the table to plane the top edges of the front and back. Test-fit and continue planing until you are satisfied with the fit.

Drawer Stops

As the name suggests, a drawer stop controls how far a drawer can slide in or out. There are two basic types depending on where they are located on a piece of furniture. Inward stops are placed near the back and keep a drawer from being pushed in too far. Outward stops are installed near the front and prevent a drawer from sliding in beyond a certain point or pulling right out.

There is a drawer stop for every piece of furniture. Inward stops are ideal for carcases with side-mounted drawers since they can be mounted at any point on the side panels. Outward stops work well for any piece, but they are simpler to install on frame-and-panel furniture.

Inward Stops: Carcase

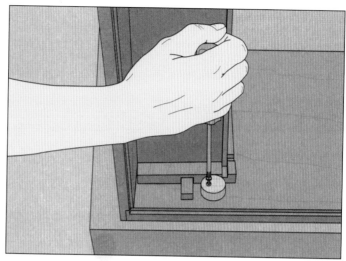

Attaching an inward stop
With a band saw or saber saw cut a 1- to 1½-inch-diameter disk from a piece of scrap wood the same thickness as the drawer sides. Bore an off-center hole in the stop, then screw the disk to a side panel near the back. Set the carcase on its side and close the drawer. Loosen the screw slightly and rotate the stop until it just touches the drawer, then tighten the screw.

Outward Stops: Carcase

Preparing the drawer
Before gluing up the drawer, cut a notch for the stop on the drawer back with a table saw. Mark cutting lines in the middle of the top edge for a 1-inch-wide notch. Set the blade high enough so that the notch will clear the stop when you install the drawer. Screw a board to the miter gauge as an extension. Aligning one of the cutting lines on the stock with the blade, butt a hand-screw against the end of the drawer back and clamp it to the extension as a stop block. Turn on the saw, hold the stock flush against the extension, and feed the two into the blade. Turn the workpiece around and cut the other side of the notch. Remove the waste in between by making repeat cuts (left).

Screwing the stop in place

Cut a drawer stop from a scrap board; make it longer and narrower than the width of the notch in the drawer back. To mount the stop, install the drawer and mark the location of the notch on the bottom of the panel or shelf under which the drawer will slide. Bore a pilot hole through the stop, then screw it in position *(right)*, aligning its edges with the lines on the carcase. Do not tighten the screw all the way. With the long edge of the stop parallel to the drawer slides, install the drawer *(inset)*. Once the stop passes completely through the notch, rotate it 90° so that its long edge is parallel to the drawer back.

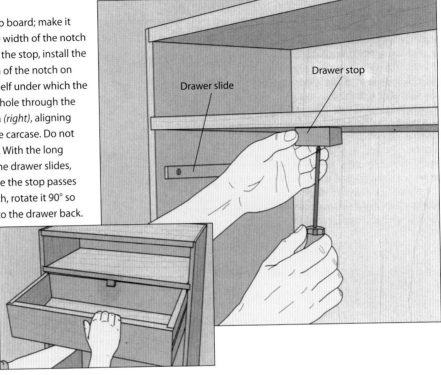

Drawer stop

Drawer slide

Outward Stops: Frame-and-Panel

Installing a stop on the front rail

Cut a drawer stop from a scrap board. It should be long enough to extend below the front rail of the cabinet when one end is attached to the rail. To mount the stop, bore a pilot hole through it near one end. With the cabinet top off, screw the stop to the middle of the rail. Leave the screw just loose enough so that you can rotate the stop out of the way. Install the drawer. Once the drawer back clears the front rail, rotate the stop 90° so that it extends below the rail *(right)*.

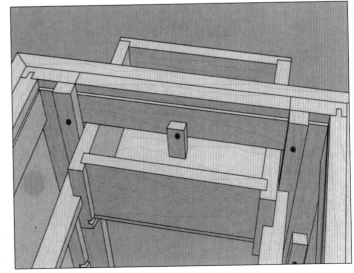

False Fronts and Hardware

Apart from their visual appeal, false fronts have practical applications in drawer-making. For the woodworker reluctant to discard a drawer that is not perfectly aligned with its opening, a properly mounted false front can provide a simple solution. Centering the front on the carcase or cabinet, rather than on the drawer, will salvage an imprecise fit. False fronts can also serve as drawer stops, but avoid exaggerating the size of the overhang. Slamming the drawer when it is filled with weighty items risks splitting the front as it strikes the cabinet.

Installing hardware on a drawer is the last—and possibly least taxing—activity in an otherwise challenging operation. Still, drawer handles and pulls need to be mounted with care. The key is to center them on the drawer front. Aligning a single-pull handle properly is fairly straightforward: Mark the diagonals across the front and install the pull where the two lines intersect. For a double-pull handle, various commercial jigs can provide fast and accurate positioning. But as shown on page 101, the job can also be done using a simple tape measure.

A drawer pull puts the finishing touch on a drawer with a false front.

Installing a False Front

Preparing the drawer
Once the drawer has been properly mounted, set it face up on a work surface and drive two brads into the drawer front, leaving their heads protruding. Make sure the brads are not located where the drawer pull will be installed. Then snip off the heads with pliers.

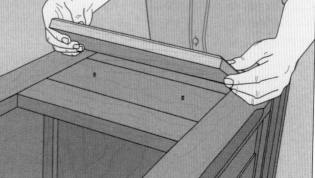

Positioning the false front
Install the drawer, then set the cabinet on its back. Cut the false front to the right size, then carefully lower it into position *(right)*. Once you are satisfied with the placement, press firmly; the pointed ends of the brads will punch impressions, allowing you to reposition the false front later when you complete the assembly.

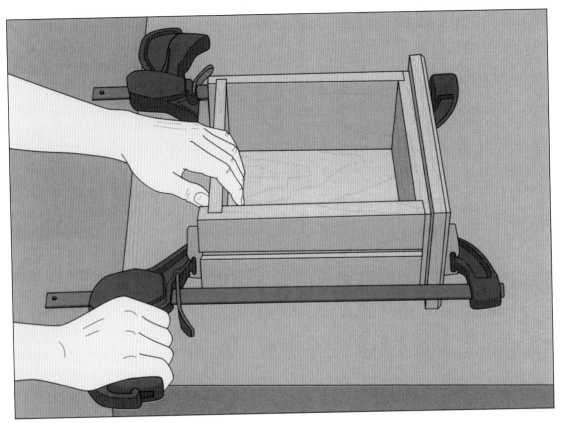

Gluing and clamping

Spread a thin layer of glue on the back of the false front. Avoid applying too much adhesive or you will end up with too much squeeze out. Place the front in position, with the two brads resting in their impressions. Hold the assembly together with bar clamps; align the bars with the drawer sides. Tighten the clamps evenly until there are no gaps between the false front and the drawer.

Shop Tip

Fastening a single-pull handle to a drawer already built

The screw supplied with a single-pull handle may not be long enough to pass through a drawer with a false front. One remedy is to countersink the screw, but if you have already assembled the drawer, a drill may not fit inside. Instead, work from the outside of the drawer. Start by boring a clearance hole through the centers of the false front and the drawer front. Then sharpen the shoulder of a spade bit slightly wider than the screw head to create a cutting edge. Feed the shank of the bit through the hole from the inside of the drawer and attach it to the drill. Switch on the tool and pull the bit toward you until the countersinking hole is the right depth.

Attaching a Drawer Handle

Marking holes for screws

Place the drawer on its back on a work surface, then mark vertical and horizontal lines across the drawer front intersecting at its center. For the double-pull handle shown below, measure the gap between its two mounting posts. Then transfer that distance to the horizontal line, making two marks the same distance from the center of the drawer (right).

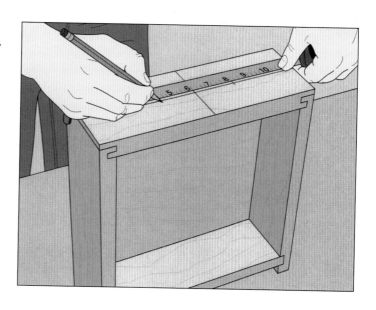

Attaching the handle

Bore clearance holes for screws at the two marked points, then apply whatever finish you have selected. To mount the handle shown, screw one mounting post to the drawer front. Slip the pull into the post, then fit the other post on the pull and screw it to the drawer front (left).

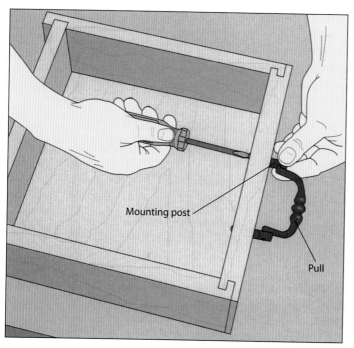

Mounting post

Pull

Doors

As a fine piece of furniture nears completion, the last major task before finishing the wood is often constructing and mounting the doors. A project within a project, assembling a door demands the same care as building the piece it accompanies. Nothing is more frustrating than seeing a carefully crafted cabinet offset by a door that is warped or ill-fitting.

In addition to providing a visual focus, doors serve the simple function of protecting the contents stored inside a piece of furniture. One of the first recorded uses in cabinet construction of a door as a physical barrier was the medieval *aumbrey*, a large cabinet used to protect food from vermin. The design of the door was primitive: a single piece of wood held in place with simple forged strap hinges.

Today's woodworkers have far more choices than their counterparts from the Middle Ages. This chapter will examine five different door types, each with its own visual appeal and application, ranging from the rustic board-and-batten door to the finely crafted frame-and-panel model. You will also learn how to build tongue-and-groove doors, glass doors and veneered-panel doors.

To some degree, the design of a piece of furniture dictates the type of door you will install on it. A board-and-batten door would be most appropriate on a simple carcase, whereas a fine period piece normally demands a frame-and-panel door. Glass doors are a good choice for a china or curio cabinet.

Since wood is prone to swelling and warping, solid doors should only be installed on relatively small pieces of furniture. With a larger cabinet—a floor-to-ceiling hutch, for example—a broad, solid door, such as the board-and-batten or tongue-and-groove door, would be more likely to buckle than would a frame-and-panel, veneered-panel, or glass door, whose construction is calculated to accommodate changes in wood movement due to shifting heat and humidity levels.

Another point to ponder is the degree of precision a door requires. A flush-mounted door permits little margin for error. A gap as little as ⅛ inch can spoil the look of an otherwise finely executed piece. Overlay doors, on the other hand, do not require the same exactness since they are designed to exceed the size of their openings.

A vast range of hardware is available for doors of all types, from rustic iron hinges reminiscent of the *aumbrey* to fine cast-brass hinges for flush doors. Most of these accessories can be purchased with one of several finishes, including black or polished iron, antique or polished brass, and chrome.

A brad driver secures a strip of molding to a door frame, sandwiching a central pane of glass between the molding and a rabbet cut into the edge of the frame.

A frame-and-panel door is hung on a cabinet with detachable cabinet hinges, which allow the door to be easily removed after installation.

Anatomy of a Door

A frame-and-panel door *(page 106)* may be built the same way as one side of a frame-and-panel cabinet. Although the door illustrated below features standard mortise-and-tenons, you can also use haunched mortise-and-tenons or cope-and-stick joints. The floating panel in the center of the door can be raised, as shown, divided into a pattern of smaller panels or inlaid. The rails and stiles have an integrated molding cut into them; for added embellishment, you may choose to cut an arch or curve into the upper rail.

The tongue-and-groove door *(page 110)* is a popular choice for modern, European-style furniture. It has stiles with grooved edges that accept tenons at the ends of the rails. The rails have grooves on their bottom edges and tongues on their tops, allowing them to interlock. Should the wood contract and the rails separate slightly, the matching tongues and grooves will hide any gaps.

The board-and-batten door *(page 112)* is assembled without glue. Rabbets are cut into the edges of the boards, which are held together by battens screwed across the back of the door. Wood plugs are used to conceal the screw heads. The glass door *(page 113)*

Board-and-Batten Door

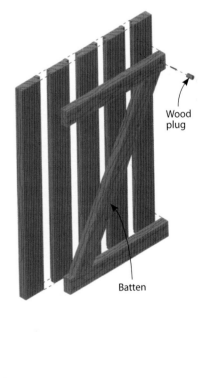

Wood plug

Batten

Tongue-and-Groove Door

Rail

Stile

Frame-and-Panel Door

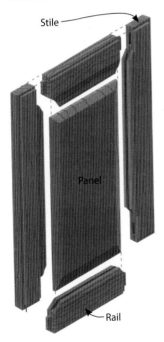

Stile

Panel

Rail

is essentially a frame-and-panel door with a glass panel rather than a panel between the rails and stiles. Standard mortise-and-tenon joints are shown in the door below. The piece of glass sits in rabbets cut along the inside edges of the frame; it is held in place by strips of molding.

The veneered-panel door *(page 115)* features a frame joined to the panel. To conceal the plate joints that connect the panel to the frame, rabbets are cut into the inside edges at the back of the frame. The panel then fits snugly into the rabbets.

Although a door is always made to fit a piece of furniture, it does not have to be sized exactly to its opening, as shown below in the drawer-mounting methods. A flush-mounted door can be difficult and time-consuming to construct because of the fine tolerances required to build and hang the door. Both lip-rabbeted and overlay doors are usually simpler to make.

The entire thickness of an overlay door projects beyond the front of a cabinet or carcase. The lip-rabbeted door has rabbets cut around its outside edges at the back so that only a part of its thickness is exposed.

Glass Door

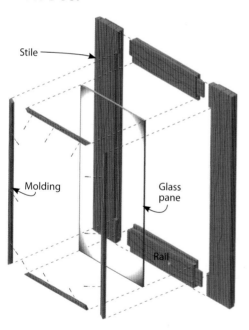

Stile

Molding

Glass pane

Rail

Veneered-Panel Door

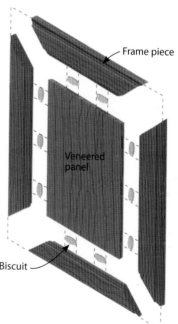

Frame piece

Veneered panel

Biscuit

Door-Mounting Methods

Flush-mounted

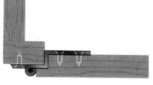

Lip-rabbeted

Overlay

Frame-and-Panel Doors

A frame-and-panel door imparts style to a piece of furniture without sacrificing durability or strength. Its solid frame construction accounts for the structural integrity. At the same time, any one of several stylistic touches can be added to make it more attractive. These include designing an arched top rail or, if the door is large enough, dividing the panel into smaller sections with horizontal cross rails and vertical mullions.

You can build a frame-and-panel door the same way you would construct a frame-and-panel assembly, using either haunched mortise-and-tenons or cope-and-stick joints *(page 50)*. This section features a door assembled with standard mortise-and-tenon joints and integrated molding. The first step is to size your stock. Make the stiles equal to the door height; the rails should be as long as the width of the door, including two tenons at each end, minus the stile width. The tenons typically are cut about ¾ inch long.

Like the frame-and-panel assembly used to build the sides of furniture, the frame-and-panel door features a sturdy frame of rails and stiles encasing a decorative floating panel.

Making a Frame-and-Panel Door

Auxiliary fence

Tenon cheek

Tenon shoulder

Cutting the tenons

Install a dado head slightly wider than the tenon length on your table saw. Attach and notch an auxiliary fence *(page 50)*, then set the width of cut equal to the length of the tenon to cut the tenon cheeks; adjust the cutting height to about one-third the thickness of the stock. Butting the rail against the fence and the miter gauge, feed the stock face down into the blades. Turn the rail over and make the same cut on the other side of the tenon. Then repeat the process at the opposite end of the rail *(left, top)* and with the second rail. To cut the tenon shoulders, set the height of the dado head at about ½ inch. With the rail flush against the fence and the miter gauge, feed the workpiece edge down into the blades. Turn the rail over and repeat on the other side of the tenon. Cut the tenon shoulders at the opposite end of the rail the same way *(left, bottom)*. Repeat the process with the second rail. To add integrated molding, fit a router with the appropriate bit and mount the tool in a router table. Cut along the inside edges of the rails and stiles as you would for making a veneered-panel door *(page 115)*.

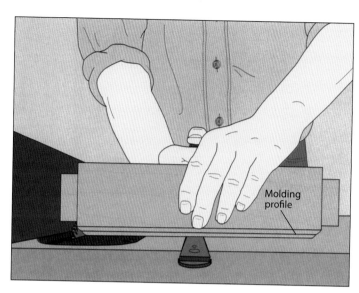

Preparing the rails for glue up

Remove the auxiliary fence and adjust the blade angle to 45°. Make a test cut in a scrap board and measure the cut end with a combination square, adjusting the blade angle if necessary. To set the width of cut, mark a line on the molded edge of a rail the same distance from the tenon shoulder as the molding width. Align the mark with the blade where it exits the table opening, then butt the fence against the rail. Adjust the blade height until one tooth just protrudes beyond the tenon shoulder. To make the cuts, butt the rail against the fence and hold it flush against the miter gauge to feed it molded-edge down into the blade. Repeat to cut the other end of the rail *(left)* and both ends of the second rail.

Molding profile

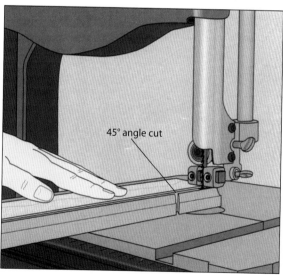

45° angle cut

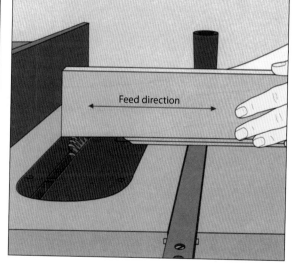

Feed direction

Readying the stiles

Before preparing the stiles for final assembly, rout a decorative stopped molding if you wish *(page 109)*. Then mark a line on the molded edge of each stile the width of a rail away from the end of the board. With the table saw blade angled at 45°, align the cutting edge with the mark and cut into the molded edge; stop the cut at the point where the molding ends and the face of the stile begins.

Next, slice off the strip of molding between the 45° cut and the end of the stile with a band saw. Then, smooth the cut edge using the table saw. Moving the rip fence out of the way, hold the stile flush against the miter gauge and slide the stock back and forth along the miter gauge *(above, right)*. Make sure you do not cut into the molded edge of the stile.

Cutting mortises

Align a rail with each stile and mark the outline of the mortises as you would when making a frame-and-panel assembly *(page 51)*. Install a mortising attachment on a drill press and clamp the stile to the fence, centering the mortise outline under the chisel and bit. Set the drilling depth to the tenon length, then make a cut at each end of the mortise before boring out the waste in between *(right)*.

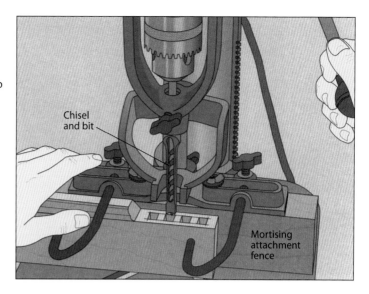

Chisel and bit

Mortising attachment fence

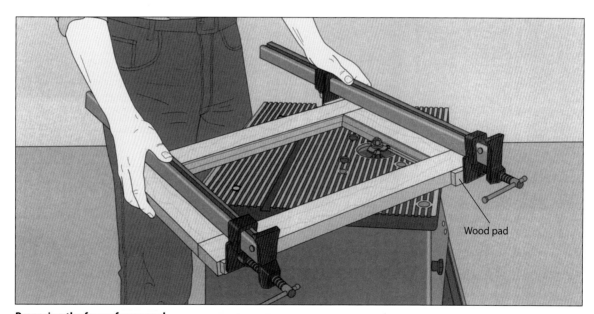

Wood pad

Preparing the frame for a panel

Assemble the rails and stiles. Then, protecting the stock with wood pads, use two bar clamps to hold the frame together securely. Fit a router with a ¼-inch three-wing slotting cutter and mount the tool in a router table. Remove the fence and set the frame on the table. Adjust the bit's cutting depth to cut the groove midway between the bottom of the frame and the edge of the molding. Gripping the bar clamps firmly, butt the inside edge of the frame against the bit near one corner, then rotate it clockwise to cut the groove along the rails and stiles *(above)*. Keep the frame flat on the table as you feed it into the bit. Make a raised panel to fit the frame *(page 55)* and then disassemble the frame.

Gluing up the door

Squeeze some glue into the mortises in the stiles and on the tenon cheeks and shoulders at the ends of the rails; also apply some adhesive on the contacting surfaces of the miter cuts in the rails and stiles. Do not add any glue to the panel grooves. Then, assemble the door and set it on two bar clamps on a work surface, aligning the rails with the bars of the clamps. To keep the clamps from falling over, prop each one on a notched wood block. Protecting the frame with wood pads, tighten the clamps just enough to fully close the joints *(right)*, then use a try square to check whether the corners of the door are at right angles. Finish tightening the clamps until glue squeezes out of the joints, checking occasionally that the corners remain square. Once the glue has dried, use a paint scraper to remove any remaining adhesive.

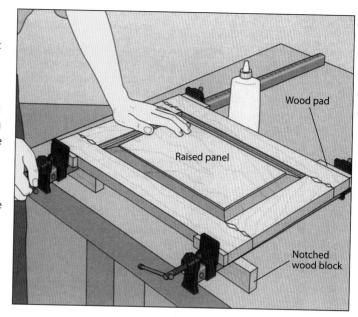

Wood pad

Raised panel

Notched wood block

Adding Decorative Molding

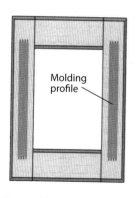

Molding profile

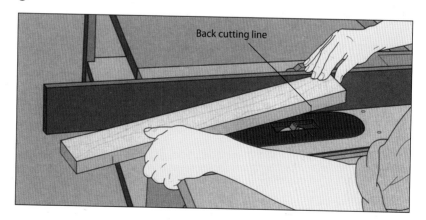

Back cutting line

Cutting molding into the stiles

Install a molding head with cutters to mill the profile of your choice; a bead design is shown *(above, left)*. Crank the cutters to ⅛ inch above the table, center one stile over them, then butt the rip fence against the stock. Mark the places on the table insert where the molding head starts and stops cutting. Then mark the points on each stile where the molding will begin and end. For each cut, hold the stile just above the molding head, aligning the front cutting line with the mark on the table insert farthest from you. Keeping the stile against the fence, lower the stock onto the blades. Once the stock is flat on the table, feed it forward while pressing it against the fence. Slide your left hand along the top of the stile and hook your fingers around the far edge of the table. Once the back cutting line reaches the mark on the table insert closest to you, lift the stile off the cutters *(above, right)*. For a deeper cut, make as many passes as necessary, raising the molding head ⅛ inch at a time.

Solid-Panel Doors

Solid-panel doors offer the same combination of strength and charm as their frame-and-panel counterparts. This section features two styles: tongue-and-groove and board-and-batten doors.

Sizing stock for a board-and-batten door is a matter of making the length of the boards equal to the door height; their combined width should equal the door width. Dimensioning stock for a tongue-and-groove door requires making the length of the stiles the same height as the door. The width of the door will be the length of the rails—without the tenons—added to the width of the stiles.

In building a board-and-batten door, some woodworkers use two horizontal battens instead of the standard Z-shaped pattern; for added strength, the two pieces are recessed in dadoes cut into the back of the door. A more elaborate method is to rout a sliding dovetail across the back and fit the batten snugly into it, securing the support piece of wood with a single screw in the center of the door.

A modern, European-style door *(front)* is assembled from rails and stiles that interlock with tenons and tongue-and-groove joints. For the more rustic board-and-batten door *(back)*, boards are joined with rabbet joints reinforced by battens screwed to the back of the door.

Making a Tongue-and-Groove Door

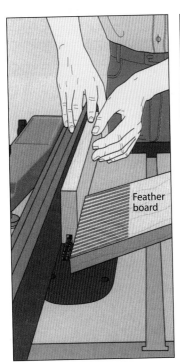

Feather board

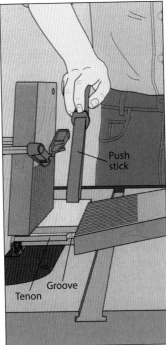

Push stick

Groove
Tenon

Milling the stock

To prepare the rails and stiles you will have to cut a series of grooves, tenons, and tongues. Begin by sawing a groove along one edge of each board, except for the bottom rail. Install a ¼-inch-wide dado head on your table saw and set the cutting height at ½ inch. Center a board edge over the blades, then butt the rip fence against the stock; clamp a featherboard to the table for support. To cut each groove, feed the stock into the blades, pressing the board against the fence *(far left)*. Then cut a tenon at the ends of each rail the same way you would for a frame-and-panel door *(page 106)*, but do not make the shoulder cut. Finally, cut a tongue along the non-grooved edge of each rail, except for the top piece. Install and notch an auxiliary fence *(page 50)*. Set the cutting height at ¼ inch, then clamp one featherboard to the fence above the dado head and install a second featherboard on the table. To cut each tongue, use a push stick to feed the rail into the dado head. Turn the board over to complete the cut *(near left)*.

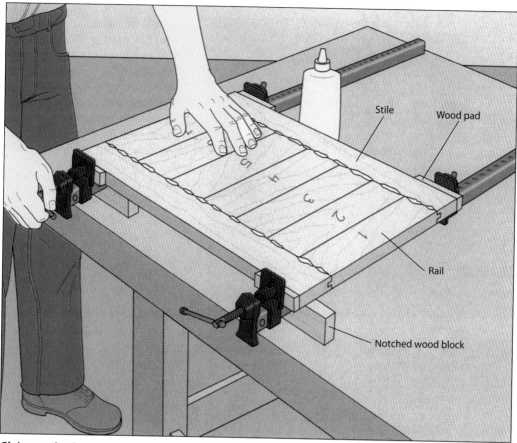

Stile

Wood pad

Rail

Notched wood block

Gluing up the door

Fit the parts of the door together, then number each rail to help you reassemble the door for final glue up. If any joint is too tight, use a wood chisel to pare some wood from the edges of the tenon or the groove, as required. Once you are satisfied with the fit, take the pieces apart and spread some glue on the tenons. Reassemble the door and place it on two bar clamps, propping them up with notched wood blocks. Protecting the stock with wood pads, tighten the clamps until glue squeezes from the joints (above). Once the adhesive has dried, remove the excess with a paint scraper.

Shop Tip

Preventing sanding scratches
Sanding the stiles of a solid-frame door may cause cross-grain scratches on the rails. An easy solution is to sand the rails first, then apply strips of masking tape to the rails, aligning the edge of the tape with the joints between the rails and stiles. Then sand the stiles.

111

Building a Board-and-Batten Door

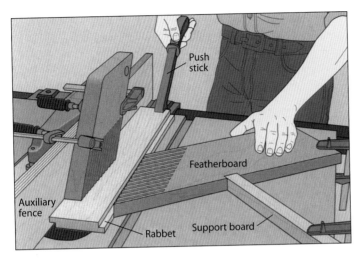

Push stick

Featherboard

Auxiliary fence

Rabbet

Support board

Cutting the rabbets

On your table saw install a dado head one-half as wide as the stock thickness. Attach and notch an auxiliary fence *(page 50)*, then set the cutting height—again, one-half the thickness of the boards. To secure the workpiece, clamp two featherboards and a support board to the table saw as shown. Feed the stock into the blades using a push stick. Then flip the board over and repeat the cut along the other edge *(left)*.

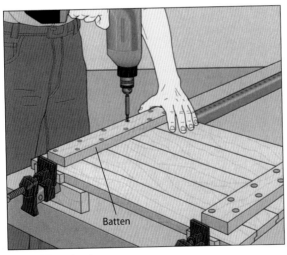

Batten

Wood plug

Assembling the door

Dry-clamp the door inside-face up using the same setup as for a tongue-and-groove door *(page 111)*. Then cut two battens slightly shorter than the door width and narrower than the door boards. Position the two pieces of wood across the top and bottom of the assembly. Fit an electric drill with a combination bit and counterbore holes for screws and wood plugs at 2-inch intervals along the battens, alternating between the top and bottom of each board. Make clearance holes except in the places where the screw will join the batten to an outside door board. Then, holding the batten square to the edge of the door, drive in each screw *(above, left)*. Cut a third batten to fit diagonally between the two already in place and screw it in position. To conceal the screws, apply a dab of glue to their heads, then insert plugs in the holes. Tap them in place with a wooden mallet *(above, right)*, then use a chisel to trim the projecting stubs flush with the door surface.

Glass Doors

Popular features of large cabinets, hutches, and shelving units, glass doors are constructed in much the same way as frame-and-panel doors *(page 106)*. The frame is held together by mortise-and-tenon joints; a decorative molding adorns its inner edges. The difference is that on a glass door the molding is not routed into the frame; instead, a rabbet is cut, then a separate glass-stop molding is nailed in place. The advantage of this design is that the molding can easily be pried off should the glass break.

In larger pieces of furniture, the door is often divided by horizontal rails and vertical mullions into several smaller panels, each holding its own pane. In addition to its aesthetic appeal, this design makes the glass less prone to breaking and also cheaper to replace.

Glass is available in various thicknesses and types. For door-making purposes, the most commonly used variety is sheet or window glass, available in thicknesses up to ¼ inch.

Glass doors solve the problem of shielding the contents of a piece of furniture from dust while still allowing them to be displayed.

Constructing a Glass Door

Wood pad

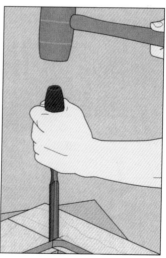

Cutting a rabbet to hold the pane of glass

Clamp the frame to a work surface, using a wood pad for protection. Then install a ⅜-inch rabbeting bit on a router and set the depth of cut to the combined thickness of the glass and the molding. Hold the tool firmly with both hands while resting the baseplate on the frame near one corner, then turn on the router and guide the bit into the inside edge of the door. Move the router clockwise along the edges *(above, left)* until the cut is completed. Square the corners with a wooden mallet and a wood chisel *(above, right)*. Make the cuts with the grain first to avoid splitting the frame.

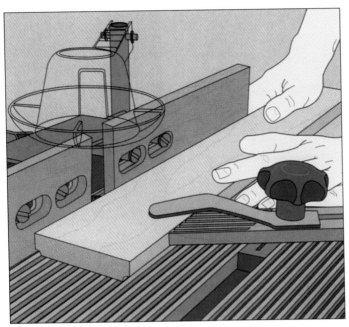

Routing the molding

Install a decorative molding bit on the router, then mount the tool in a router table. Choose a board long enough to produce the length of molding you need. To secure the stock, install two featherboards on the router table—one pressing the workpiece toward the fence and one pressing down directly above the router. (Here, the upper featherboard has been removed for clarity.) Turn on the tool and feed the workpiece into the bit while keeping the board flush against the fence. Finish the pass using a push stick. Repeat the step to rout a second molding in the opposite edge of the workpiece *(left)*, then rip the two from the stock with a table saw. Saw the molding to the proper length, making 45° miter cuts at the ends of each piece. Cut and fit one piece at a time, making sure you align the miter cuts with the corners of the rabbets.

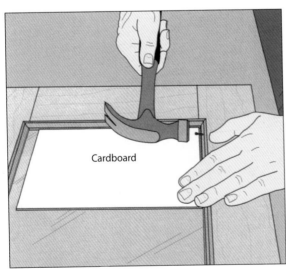

Cardboard

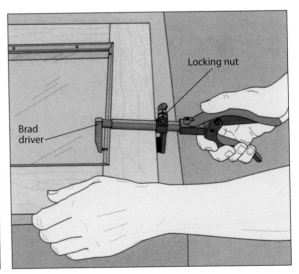

Locking nut

Brad driver

Final assembly

Set the frame and the glass on a work surface, then place the molding in position. Bore a pilot hole every 2 inches using an electric drill fitted with a small finishing nail with the head snipped off. Then drive the brads in place using either a hammer or a brad driver. With the hammer, hold the molding flush against the frame of the door; use a piece of cardboard to protect the glass *(above, left)*. To use a brad driver, insert a brad into the pilot hole, then position the jaws and tighten the locking nut. Holding the frame steady, squeeze the jaws to set the nail *(above, right)*.

Veneered-Panel Doors

As ornamental as the frame-and-panel door, the veneered-panel door is much simpler to make. First of all, it does not require mortise-and-tenon joints. In fact, the frame adds no strength to the door at all; the four sides are simply mitered at each end. The assembly is held together by biscuit joints that affix it to a plywood panel, which serves as the structural backbone of the door.

The veneered plywood is formed by up to nine plies of thin veneer glued together. The outer skin is typically ½₈ inch thick for hardwoods and ⅒₀ inch thick for softwoods.

Since plywood is not affected by humidity, no allowance has to be made for changes in the size of the panel. Therefore, it does not need to have a bevel cut along its edge to fit into a groove on the frame. The plywood simply rests in a rabbet cut in the frame.

The panel of a veneered-panel door—with its typically dark-hued wood—offers a visual contrast to the lighter-colored frame.

Making a Veneered-Panel Door

Routing a molding in the frame pieces

Rip the four frame pieces to width, then crosscut them slightly longer than their finished length. Fit a router with a decorative molding bit, then install the machine in a router table. For each cut, feed the workpiece good-face down into the bit (above), using a featherboard to brace the stock against the fence and a push stick to complete the pass.

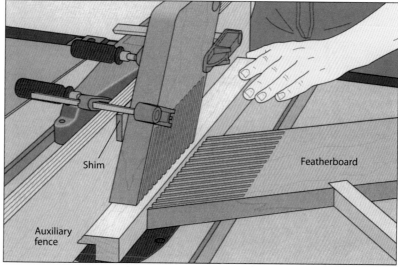

Shim

Featherboard

Auxiliary fence

Cutting a rabbet and sizing the stock

Cut a rabbet just as you would to make a board-and-batten door (page 112). Set the cutting height at the thickness of the panel; the width should be one-half the stock thickness. Clamp featherboards to the saw table to support the workpiece. Insert a shim between the vertical featherboard and the fence to keep the pressure off the rabbeted part of the stock. Feed the workpiece good-face up into the dado head (above). Then cut the frame pieces to size, making 45° miter cuts at each end. Dry-assemble the frame, then cut the panel to fit. Identify the panel edges and their mating frame pieces to help you correctly assemble the door for glue-up.

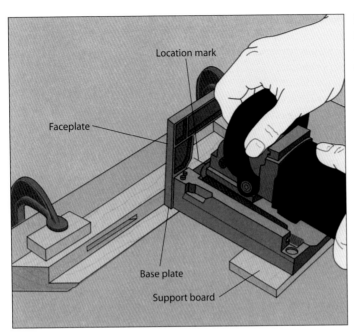

Location mark

Faceplate

Base plate

Support board

Preparing the frame and panel for glue-up

Mark a line across the panel and the frame pieces about 4 inches from each edge and at 6-inch intervals in between. Disassemble the door and clamp one frame piece to a work surface, protecting the stock with wood pads. Adjust the depth of cut on a plate joiner, then set the tool's base plate on the bottom of the rabbet in the frame piece. With a support board under the joiner to keep it level, align the guide line on the tool with a slot location mark. Holding the joiner with both hands, cut a groove at each mark *(left)*. Repeat for the other frame pieces, then cut the mating slots in the panel the same way.

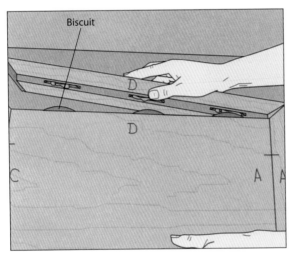

Biscuit

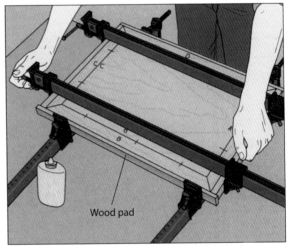

Wood pad

Gluing up the door

Once all the slots have been cut, glue up the door. Set the frame pieces and the panel good-face up on a work surface and squeeze glue into each slot, inserting biscuits as you go. To prevent the wafers from expanding before everything is put together, assemble the door as quickly as possible, fitting the frame pieces to the panel *(above, left)*. Next, set the door on two bar clamps on a work surface. With wood pads protecting the frame, tighten the clamps just enough to close the joints. Install two more clamps across the top of the door, placing them perpendicular to the first two. Finish tightening until glue squeezes out of the joints *(above, right)*. Once the adhesive has dried, remove any excess with a paint scraper.

Hanging a Door

Cast in metals ranging from wrought-iron to brass, door hinges come in a wide array of styles to complement virtually any door. Most fit into one of four basic categories shown at right. Clock-case hinges are best suited to doors that overlay their opening. Commonly used for flush-mounted doors, butt hinges typically sit in shallow mortises cut into the door and case. Surface-mounted hinges are ideal for imparting an antique or rustic look to a door. Concealed hinges, such as the European cabinet hinge, are completely hidden when the door is closed.

Before installing the hinges, read the manufacturer's instructions regarding hinge placement. If you are working with fine woods, tap the stock for brass machine screws after drilling pilot holes to reduce the chance of splitting. A spot of glue in the hole will improve the holding ability of the screw.

Door hinges

Clock-case hinge
Pivots on a pin, which allows the door to be lifted off.

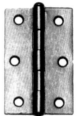

Butt hinge
Available in iron or brass.

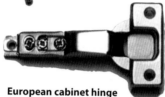

European cabinet hinge
Commonly used in kitchen cabinets; spring-mounted. Can be adjusted after installation to correct minor mounting inaccuracies.

Surface-mounted hinge
A decorative hinge installed on the outside face of flush doors.

Installing European Cabinet Hinges

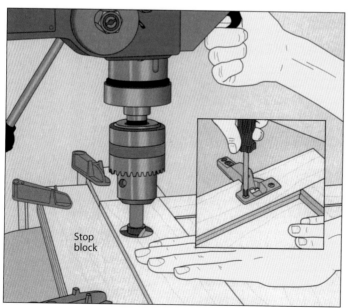

Stop block

Attaching the hinge bodies

On your drill press, install a Forstner bit the width of the hinge body—typically, 35mm. Set the door outside-face down on the machine's table, then align the bit with one of the two marks for the hinges. If you are hanging several doors, clamp stop blocks against the edge and end of the door. Set the drilling depth to the thickness of the hinge body. Holding the door flush against the stop blocks, feed the bit into the door (left). If you are working with more than one door, drill the other ones, too. Then align the mark at the other end of the door under the drill bit. Reposition the stop blocks and bore the hole; repeat for any other doors. Set the door on a work surface and screw the hinge body in place (inset).

Reference line

Mounting plate

Aligning and attaching the mounting plates

Have a helper hold the door in its open position against the case. Extend the hinge arms to butt the mounting plates against the panel. Mark a reference line around the plates, then unscrew them from the hinge arms. Place the plates in position on the panel inside the case and drive in the screws *(left)*.

Hinge arm

Hanging the door

Slide the arms onto the mounting plates and screw in place *(right)*. Close the door and check its position on the case. You can adjust the height, depth or lateral position of the door by loosening or tightening the adjustment screws on the hinge arms.

118

Attaching Butt Hinges

Routing mortises for the hinges

Secure the door in handscrews and clamp them in place on a work surface. Position one of the hinges on the door edge, making sure that the pin projects over the edge. Mark the outline of the hinge leaf with a pencil. Repeat for the second hinge. Install a straight-cutting bit on a router and set the depth of cut to the thickness of a hinge leaf. Protecting the door with wood pads, clamp a board to the door as an edge guide. Position the router bit slightly above the door edge just inside the outline. Gripping the handles firmly, turn on the tool and lower the bit into the stock. Once the base plate sits squarely on the door *(right)*, guide the bit in a circular motion around the outline. Use a wood chisel to square the edges of the mortises, then screw the hinges to the door.

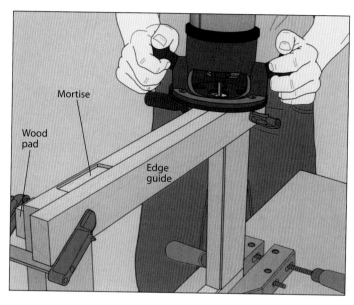

Mortise

Wood pad

Edge guide

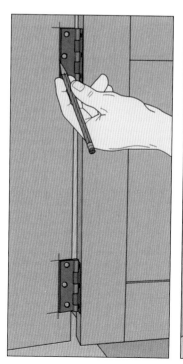

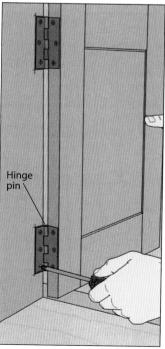

Hinge pin

Hanging the door

While a helper holds the door against the case in its open position, butt the hinge leaves against the inside face of the case. Making sure that the hardware's pin projects beyond the edge of the panel, use a pencil to outline the hinge leaf *(far left)*. Place the case on its side and rout the mortises, following the same procedures described above. Then screw the hinges to the case *(near left)*.

Installing Clock-Case Hinges

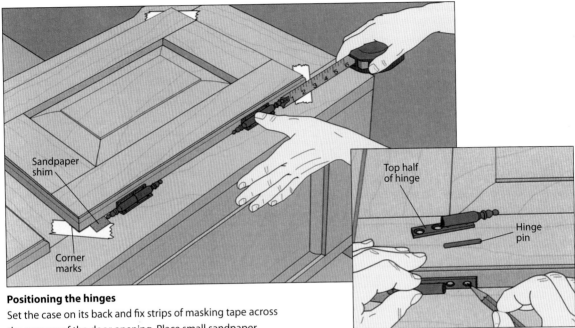

Sandpaper
shim

Corner
marks

Top half
of hinge

Hinge
pin

Positioning the hinges

Set the case on its back and fix strips of masking tape across
the corners of the door opening. Place small sandpaper
shims on top of the pieces of tape, then set the door in place.
Once you are satisfied with the positioning, mark the door
corners on the tape with a pencil. Next, butt the hinges
against the edge of the door; use a tape measure to make
sure that they are equally spaced from the top and bottom
of the door *(above)*. Holding the upper half of the hinge in
place, slip off the bottom half and the hinge pin. Then mark
the screw holes on the door edge *(inset)*.

Mounting the hinges on the door

Secure the door to a work surface
with handscrews and clamps, then
bore pilot holes at each marked
point. Hold the top half of each
hinge square to the door edge and
screw it in place *(right)*.

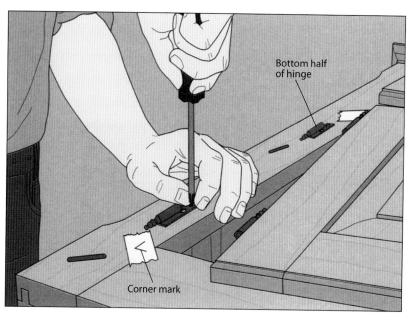

Bottom half
of hinge

Corner mark

Hanging the door

Reassemble the hinge and reposition the door on the case. Check that the corners of the door are aligned with the marks on the masking tape. Holding the bottom half of one of the hinges, disassemble the hinge and move the door aside, then mark the screw holes on the case. Repeat for the other hinge. Bore pilot holes, then screw the bottom half of each hinge to the case *(left)*. Remove the shims and tape strips, insert the pin in the bottom part of the hinge and then place the door on the case.

Adding Surface-Mounted Hinges

Mounting the hinges

With the door good-face up on a work surface, position the hinges on the door, making sure that the pins extend just beyond the edge of the door. Also check that the hinges are the same distance from the top and bottom of the door. Mark the screw holes on the door with a pencil, then bore pilot holes. Screw the hinges to the door. To mount the hinges to the piece of furniture, set the case on its back. Hold the door in the case and place a piece of sandpaper between the two to serve as a shim. With the hinge pin centered over the edge of the door opening, mark the screw holes on the case. Bore pilot holes and drive in the screws *(right)*.

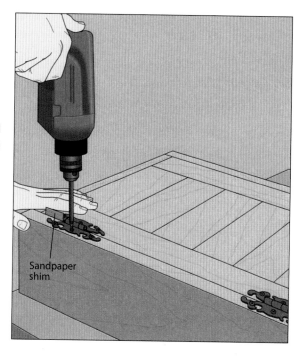

Sandpaper
shim

Legs

Like their counterparts in human anatomy, legs in cabinet construction serve mainly as supports. Whatever the style of legs, the challenges of making them are the same: shape and proportion must be perfectly in balance with the rest of the piece of furniture and the leg must provide adequate support. The goal is to achieve a balance between strength and beauty.

This chapter will show you how to make four popular leg types: cabriole, tapered, octagonal, and square legs. Several methods of attaching legs are also presented. These leg types and joinery techniques offer attractive alternatives for a wide range of furniture styles.

Among the most distinctive of designs for legs, the cabriole is best suited to traditional styles of furniture, such as Queen Anne and Hepplewhite. But as American furnituremakers have shown since the 19th Century, accomplished craftsmanship can keep this design fresh and appropriate. As you will see, the cabriole leg does have certain design requirements that should be respected (page 126). The characteristic contours of the leg are more than simply random shapes. Incorporating animal profiles in the design, for example, has always been a feature. The Italian word *capriolare*, an antecedent of the English term, refers to an animal leaping into the air, an action which many versions of the leg are calculated to suggest.

In general, legs should be attached to furniture with the strongest of joinery techniques (page 135), such as the mortise-and-tenon or the dowel joint. Another option is leg hardware, which is commercially available or easily made in the shop. This alternative allows a leg to be detached.

For most leg projects, you will need thicker stock than is commonly available. You can either order proper-sized wood from a specialized supplier, or make your own leg blanks from thinner stock, using a process called face-gluing. Start by preparing the stock slightly larger than the final size of the leg: To make a leg whose finished dimensions will be 3 by 3 by 29 inches, cut three 1¼-inch by 3¼-inch by 30-inch boards. To ensure a seamless fit, joint the mating surfaces. Then glue up the boards face to face, alternating the end grain of the pieces and arranging the stock to maximize grain and color.

The process is identical to edge-gluing boards into panels (page 22), except that more clamps should be used. Before cutting into your leg blank, joint a face and an edge to create two surfaces that are at a 90° angle to one another, then use the planer or the table saw to bring the blank to its final width and thickness.

The cabriole leg harkens back to the time-honored art of shaping wood with hand tools. Here, the leg's unmistakable contours are revealed or smoothed by a spokeshave, traditional cousin of the hand plane.

A router plows a rectangular groove for an inlay into a square leg.

Anatomy of a Cabriole Leg

The illustration below shows one of the common ways a leg—in this case, a cabriole leg—is joined to a piece of furniture, such as a simple carcase. Before attaching the leg to the rails, you will need to cut a rabbet along the top of the rails. After assembly, the top of the leg is trimmed to the level of the rabbet. Next, glue is applied to the rabbets, the notches and the contacting surfaces of the carcase, and the casework is seated on the leg-and-rail assembly. The weight of the piece eliminates the need for clamping.

There are many ways of joining legs to rails, including the four techniques shown opposite and featured in this chapter. The mortise-and-tenon and dowel joints are two alternatives designed to last the life of a piece of furniture. If you choose the mortise-and-tenon, remember that the tenons are always cut at the ends of the rails, while the mortises are always chiseled out of the legs.

Whether you buy hardware for attaching the legs or build your own in the shop, it offers the strength and durability of traditional joinery, with the added benefit of ease of disassembly—an option impossible with a glue joint.

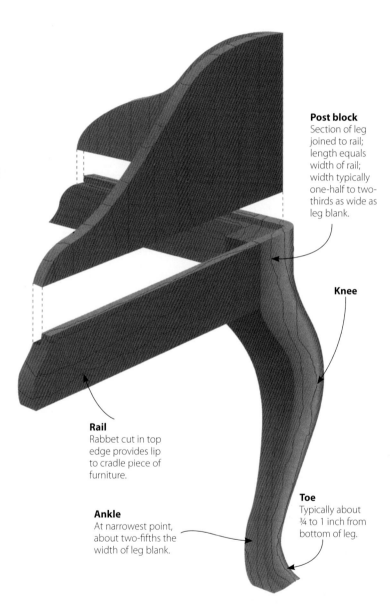

Post block
Section of leg joined to rail; length equals width of rail; width typically one-half to two-thirds as wide as leg blank.

Knee

Rail
Rabbet cut in top edge provides lip to cradle piece of furniture.

Toe
Typically about ¾ to 1 inch from bottom of leg.

Ankle
At narrowest point, about two-fifths the width of leg blank.

Leg-to-Rail Joints

Dowel joint

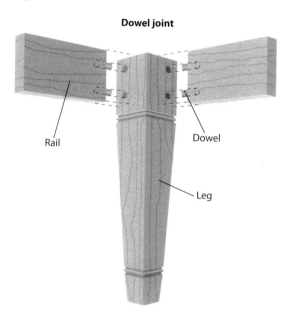

Rail

Dowel

Leg

Mortise-and-tenon joint

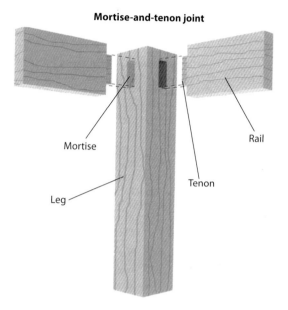

Mortise

Rail

Leg

Tenon

Leg hardware

Commercial hardware

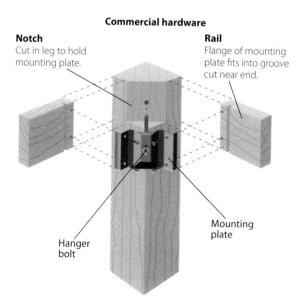

Notch
Cut in leg to hold mounting plate.

Rail
Flange of mounting plate fits into groove cut near end.

Hanger bolt

Mounting plate

Shop-made hardware

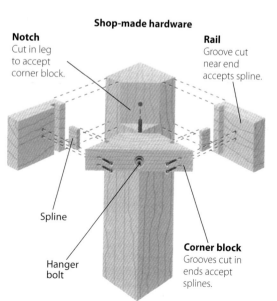

Notch
Cut in leg to accept corner block.

Rail
Groove cut near end accepts spline.

Spline

Hanger bolt

Corner block
Grooves cut in ends accept splines.

125

Cabriole Legs

Although its origins can be traced back to woodworkers of classical times in China, Egypt, Greece and Rome, the cabriole leg has become a ubiquitous fixture of Western furniture in the past 200 years. The best known designs include the staid Queen Anne leg with its spoon-shaped foot and the ornate ball-and-claw foot of the American colonial design. Due to the leg's widespread popularity, every generation has added its own touches or varied old ones, so that there is no standard pattern. Designs range from legs with exaggerated curves to others that are almost knee-less and virtually straight. The most common element of cabriole legs is the S-shaped curve, which is meant to suggest the grace and elegance of a horse's leg.

The design shown below will yield an attractive, well-proportioned leg strong and stable enough to support a piece of furniture. You can alter the pattern to suit your own project or copy the design of an existing leg that appeals to you. However, do not exaggerate the curves too much or you risk making the leg unstable. Before cutting into the block of wood, perform this simple test on your design: Draw a straight line from the top of the leg to the bottom; the line should fall within the leg outline at every point.

A cabriole leg.

Making a Cabriole Leg

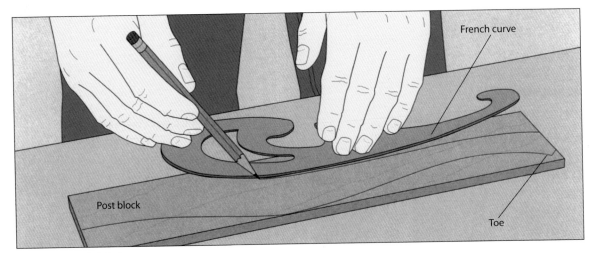

French curve

Post block

Toe

Designing a cabriole leg

For a template, cut a piece of stiff cardboard or hardboard to the same length and width as your leg blanks. To draw the leg, start by outlining the post block. Make its length equal to the width of the rail that will be attached to the leg; the width should be adequate to accept the tenon of the rail (one-half to two-thirds the width of the stock is typical). Next, sketch the toe; for a leg of the proportions shown, it should be about ¾ to 1 inch from the bottom of the leg. Then draw a curve on the front of the leg from the toe to the ankle using a trench curve; at its narrowest point, the diameter of the ankle should be about two-fifths the stock width. Move on to the knee, sketching a gentle curve from the post block to the front edge of the template about 2 to 3 inches below the block. Then join the knee to the ankle with a relatively straight line. Complete the outline at the back of the leg, connecting the bottom of the leg with the back of ankle. Then sketch a curve from the ankle to the bottom of the post block (above). Experiment with the outline until you have a satisfactory design.

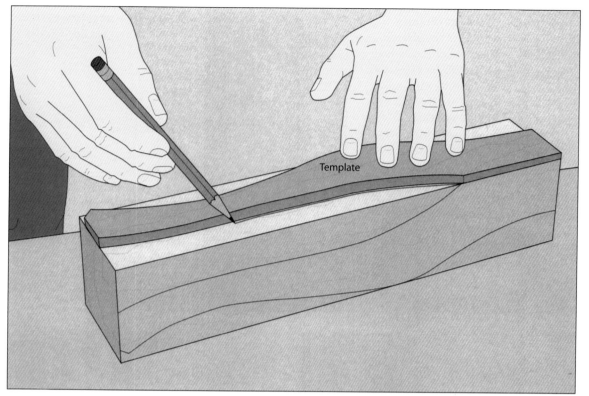

Template

Shop Tip

Copying the design of a cabriole leg

To transfer the contours of an existing leg onto a template, use this shop-made tracing guide. Cut a 2-inch cube from a scrap block, then use your table saw to form a V in one edge. Saw off the bottom half of the wedge. Remove the cartridge from a ball-point pen and use epoxy glue to bond it to the cube just to one side of the V; tape the cartridge to the block while the glue is drying. To use the guide, hold the template flat against one side of the leg. Then, guide the pen along the back and front of the leg, making sure the point of the V rides against the edge of the leg.

Transferring the design to the leg blank

Cut out your template on a band saw, then sand the edges up to the marked outline. Hold the template flat on one of the inside faces of the leg blank, making sure that the ends of the template and the blank are aligned and that the back of the post block is flush with the inside edge of the block of wood. Trace along the edges of the template to outline the leg. Turn the blank over and repeat the procedure on the other inside face *(above)*. At this point, some woodworkers prefer to make preparations for the joinery before cutting the leg. (It is easier to clamp and cut a mortise in a rectangular leg blank, for example, than to carry out the same procedures in a leg with pronounced contours.) Other woodworkers cut the leg first and then do the joinery.

127

Making the cuts on one face of the leg

Set the leg blank on the band saw table with one of the marked outlines facing up and the bottom of the leg pointing away from you. Aligning the saw blade just to the waste side of the marked line for the back of the leg, feed the stock into the blade. Turn off the saw about halfway through the cut and remove the workpiece. Then cut along the same line from the opposite end. To avoid detaching the waste piece from the blank and losing the marked outline on the adjacent face, stop the cut about ½ inch from the first kerf, leaving a short bridge between the two cuts. Retract the workpiece, then cut along the line for the front of the leg *(right)*.

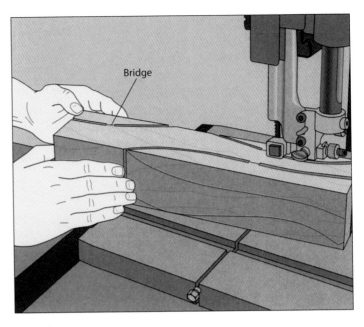

Bridge

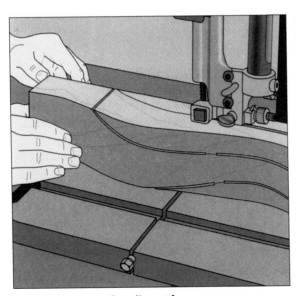

Making the cuts on the adjacent face

Turn over the blank so that the marked outline on its adjacent side is facing up. Cut along the marked lines, beginning at the foot *(above)*. This time, complete the cut, letting the waste fall away.

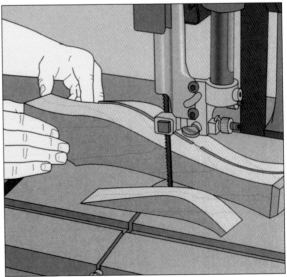

Cutting the bridges

Rotate the blank so that the first face you cut faces up. With the saw off, slide the blank forward to feed the blade into the kerf at the back of the leg. Turn on the saw and cut through the bridge to release the waste piece *(above)*. Then cut through the bridge between the kerfs at the front of the leg.

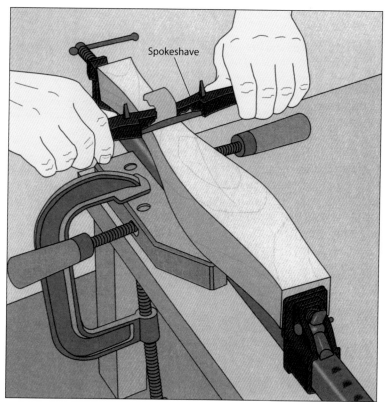

Spokeshave

Shaping and smoothing the leg

To finish shaping the cabriole leg and to remove any blemishes left by the band saw blade, smooth its surfaces with a spokeshave, followed by a rasp and sandpaper. In preparation for this smoothing process, secure the leg in a bar clamp and fix the clamp to a work surface with a handscrew and a C clamp as shown. Holding a spokeshave with both hands at the top of a curved edge of the leg, pull the tool slowly toward you, cutting a thin shaving and following the grain *(left)*. Repeat until the surface is smooth. Turn the leg in the bar clamp to clean up the other edges. To smooth an area that the spokeshave cannot reach, use the rasp. The tool works best when pushed diagonally across the grain. Finish the job with sandpaper, using progressively finer-grit papers until the surface is smooth.

Shop Tip

Sanding a cabriole leg

Smoothing the curved surfaces of a cabriole leg using only a sheet of sandpaper or a sanding block risks creating bumps or valleys or flattening out the curves if excessive pressure is applied. Use a shop-made sanding pad that will follow the contours of the leg. Wrap a sheet of sandpaper around a thick sponge that you can comfortably grip and hold the paper around the sponge as you smooth the leg. Even with firm hand pressure, there is no risk of oversanding.

Tapered and Octagonal Legs

Cabinetmakers taper legs strictly for visual effect. A taper adds no strength, but neither does it take any away. Its principal effect is to reduce the stolid heaviness of a leg, imparting a sleek appearance to furniture as diverse as traditional English and contemporary Scandinavian designs.

A leg can be tapered on one inside face, on two outside faces, or, as illustrated below and on page 129, on all four sides. Before settling on the amount of taper for a leg—expressed in either degrees or inches per foot—you can evaluate the visual impact of the finished product without cutting into your leg blank. Experiment with different tapers by simply masking off the part to be cut away with a piece of light-colored cardboard. There are no prescriptions for the ideal amount of taper, but as a general rule, the thicker and longer the leg, the greater the angle.

Another option well-suited to many furniture styles is the octagonal leg. Despite its appearance of intricacy, it is easy to create using a table saw, as shown on page 132. For either style of leg, be sure to sand the stock thoroughly before preparing it for joinery.

Cut on a table saw fitted with a molding head and cutters, a bead profile adds a distinctive decorative touch to this tapered leg.

Jointing a Tapered Leg

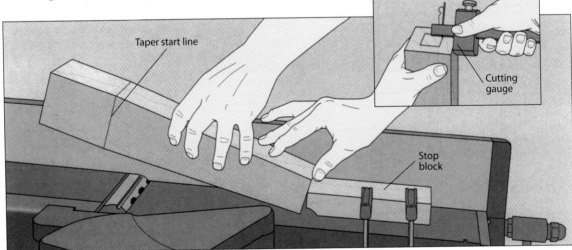

Taper start line

Cutting gauge

Stop block

Setting up and starting the cut

Use a cutting gauge to outline the taper on the bottom end of the leg blank (inset). Then mark lines on the four faces of the stock near the opposite end to indicate where the taper will begin. Install a clamp on the jointer's infeed table to hold the guard out of the way during the operation. Set the depth of cut for ⅛ inch and, holding the blank against the fence, align the taper start line with the front of the outfeed table.

Butt a stop block against the leg as shown and clamp it to the infeed table. To start each pass, carefully lower the blank onto the cutterhead while holding it firmly against the fence with your left hand (above). Straddle the fence with your right hand, using your thumb to keep the blank flush against the stop block. Make sure both hands are over the infeed side of the cutterhead.

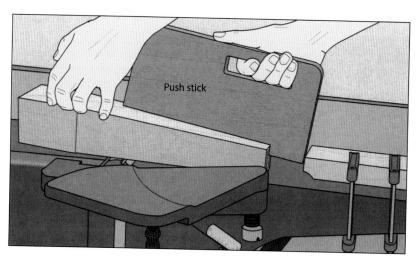

Jointing the taper

Feed the leg across the cutterhead with a push stick, pushing down on the trailing end of the stock while pressing it flush against the fence *(left)*. Keep your left hand away from the cutterhead. Make as many passes as necessary until you have trimmed the stock down to the taper outline, then repeat the process to shape the remaining faces.

Push stick

Adding Decorative Molding

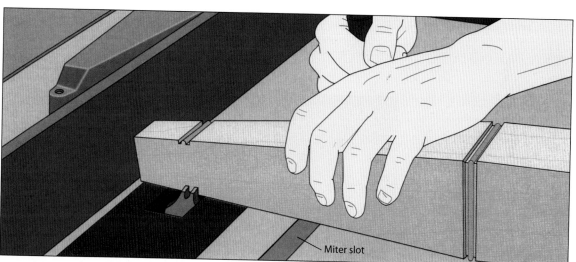

Miter slot

Cutting molding into a leg

On your table saw install a molding head with the appropriate cutters; a bead profile is shown. Mark a cutting line for each molding on one face of the leg, then hold the leg against the miter gauge. For a tapered leg, you will have to adjust the angle of the gauge. Use a carpenter's square to make sure that the square part of the leg is perpendicular to the miter slot. Crank the cutters to ⅛ inch above the table and align one of the cutting lines with the molding head.

Then butt the rip fence against the leg. To cut the first molding, press the leg firmly against the miter gauge and the fence, while feeding the stock into the cutters. Repeat the cut on the adjacent face, then continuing in the same manner until you have cut the molding on all four sides. For a deeper cut, make as many passes as necessary, raising the molding head ⅛ inch at a time. **(Caution: Blade guard removed for clarity.)**

Shaping an Octagonal Leg

Setting up the cut
Unplug the table saw, crank the blade to its highest setting and adjust the cutting angle to 45°. Move the rip fence to the left-hand side of the blade. Lay one face of the leg blank on the blade with a corner resting on the saw table, then butt the fence against the stock *(left)*.

Cutting the leg
Butt the stock against the rip fence a few inches in front of the blade. Adjust the cutting height until one tooth just protrudes beyond the face of the workpiece. To make the first cut, feed the blank into the blade, straddling the fence with your left hand. Rotate the leg 90° clockwise and repeat the cut on the adjacent face. Continue in this same manner until all the sides are cut.

Inlays and Detailing

Adding inlay to a leg can transform an easily overlooked square or octagonal block of wood into the eye-catching focus of a piece of furniture. Whether the goal is to create a contrast with the leg stock or to complement a leg's outlines, you can choose from a wide variety of inlay materials, including metals, wood veneers, marquetry, and—as shown below and on page 134—solid hardwood. Each type of material can be prepared in the shop, but most are also available in various diameters at fine woodworking stores.

Standard practice is to rout a groove for an inlay from the top to the bottom of a leg. However, before cutting into your leg, hold pieces of inlay of different lengths up against it and select an arrangement that produces the best effect.

Another decorative option is to rout a molding into a leg. Although it does not stand out as boldly as inlay, molding can add its own distinctive touch to a piece of furniture. You can also install a molding cutterhead on your table saw and carve out a pattern, much as you would on a door frame *(page 109)*.

An inlay of marquetry creates a vivid counterpoint to the understated grain pattern of an octagonal leg.

Legs

Adding Inlay to a Leg

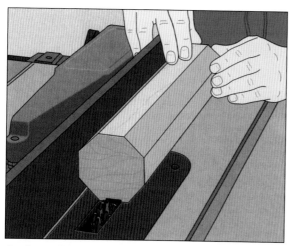

Stop block

Edge guide

Cutting and routing grooves

To cut a straight groove, use your table saw with a dado head the same width as the inlay; set the cutting height to slightly less than its thickness. Make a cut in a scrap board and test the fit; adjust the width and cutting height of the blades, if necessary. Next, mark a line for the groove on the leading end of the leg and align it with the dado head. Butt the rip fence against the stock, then feed it into the blades *(above, left)*. To make a groove with more than one straight cut, use a router.

Start by securing all four edges of the leg with stop blocks. Then install a straight-cutting bit on your router and set the cutting depth to slightly less than the thickness of the inlay. Outline the groove on the leg, then adjust the tool's edge guide to align the bit with one of the lines that run across the grain. Gripping the router firmly, cut the groove, moving the tool against the direction of bit rotation. Repeat to cut the other grooves, then square the corners with a chisel.

Setting the inlay in the groove

Cut the inlay to fit in the groove with a table saw, a backsaw and miter box, or a wood chisel. For the rectangular groove shown, make 45° miter cuts at the ends of the inlay pieces. It is easiest to cut and fit one piece at a time, making sure you align the miter cuts with the corners of the grooves. Next, spread a little glue in the slot and on the mitered ends of the inlay pieces. Insert one strip at a time, tapping it gently with a wooden mallet *(right)*. Once the glue has dried, gently sand the leg to remove any excess adhesive and to trim the inlay perfectly flush with the surface of the wood. If you are using metal inlay, cut it with a hacksaw and sand the surfaces that will contact the groove to improve adhesion. Then bond the strip in place with epoxy glue.

Detailing the Surface of a Leg

Routing detailing

Hold the leg in place with stop blocks screwed to a work surface. Mark lines on the leg for the beginning and end of the cut. Then install a decorative bit on your router; a cove bit with a ball-bearing pilot is shown. Set a cutting depth appropriate to the profile you want to make, then align the bit with the start line. Gripping the router with both hands, guide the bit along the corner of the leg against the direction of bit rotation, stopping when you reach the end line. Repeat to rout the detailing on the other corner of the leg *(left)*.

Leg Joinery

This section features two time-tested methods for permanently joining legs to the rails of a piece of furniture: the mortise-and-tenon joint and the dowel joint. Two more contemporary ways are also featured; both involve using knock-down leg hardware—suitable for furniture that must be taken apart and reassembled periodically.

To some extent, the type of leg will dictate the way you join it to the rails. You would be unlikely, for example, to use a hanger bolt to fix a cabriole leg to a fine frame-and-panel cabinet. A mortise-and-tenon joint would be a more appropriate choice.

There are several techniques for making the mortise-and-tenon. You can use a table saw to cut the tenons (page 106); the mortises can be bored with a router (page 52) or a drill press (page 108). You may also choose to use hand tools. Whatever method you choose, the strength of the joint will be enhanced by its large gluing area.

As a rule of thumb, the length of the tenon should generally be about three-quarters the thickness of the leg. The tenon is typically about one-third as thick as the rail, but many woodworkers base the tenon's thickness instead on the width of the chisel with which they will chop out the mortise.

The tenon at the end of a rail fits snugly in a mortise cut out of a square leg, creating a sturdy, long-lasting joint.

Legs

Back to **Basics**

Hand-Cut Mortise-and-Tenon Joints

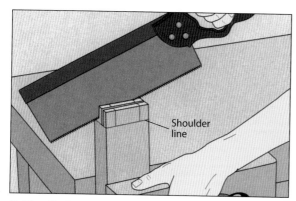

Shoulder line

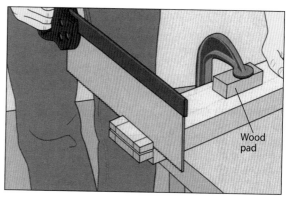

Wood pad

Cutting the tenons

Outline the tenons on the rails, then secure one of the workpieces end-up in a vise. Cut along the lines on the end of the rail with a backsaw; tilt the saw forward and cut to the shoulder line of the tenon (above, left). Then complete the cut with the saw level. To remove the waste from the tenon cheeks, clamp the rail face-up to a work surface, protecting the stock with a wood pad. Cut along the shoulder line on the face of the rail; turn over the stock and repeat the operation on the other side (above, right). To cut away the waste on the edges of the tenon, secure the rail end-up again and saw along the edges of the tenon to the shoulder line. Finally, clamp the rail edge-up and cut through the shoulder lines on both edges of the rail. Repeat to cut the tenons at the other end of the rail and at both ends of the other rails.

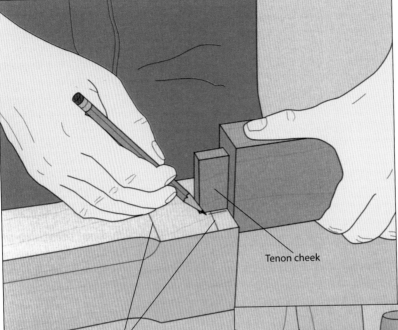

Outlining the mortises

Mark mortise outlines on each leg in two steps, using one of the rail tenons as a guide. First, hold the cheek of the tenon flush against the leg, with the top of the rail aligned with the end of the leg. Draw a pencil along the edges of the tenon to outline the length of the mortise, then use a try square to continue the lines across the leg. To mark the width of the mortise, hold the edge of the tenon centered flush against the leg *(left)*. Extend the marks along the leg until the two outlines intersect. Repeat to mark another mortise on the adjacent face of the leg for the adjoining rail.

Tenon cheek

Mortise length marks

Mortising chisel

Wood pad

Chiseling the mortises

For each of the mortises, clamp the leg to a work surface, protecting the stock with a wood pad. Then, starting at one end of an outline, hold a mortising chisel square to the face of the leg and strike it with a wooden mallet. Use a chisel the same width as the tenon and be sure that the beveled side of the blade is facing the waste. Make another cut ⅛ inch from the first. Continue until you reach the other end of the outline, levering out the waste to a depth that slightly exceeds the length of the tenon. Test-fit the tenon and widen or deepen the mortise as required.

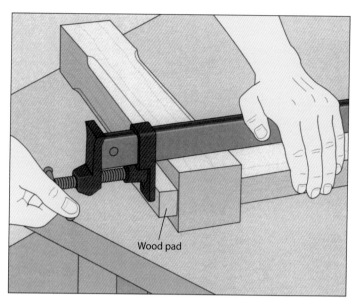

Wood pad

Gluing up the leg and rail

Spread a little glue in the mortise and on the cheeks and shoulders of the tenon. Fit the two together, making sure that the tops of the rail and the leg are flush. Protecting the leg with a wood pad, hold the joint together with a bar clamp. Align the bar of the clamp with the rail, then tighten it until a bead of glue squeezes out of the joint. Once the adhesive has dried, remove any excess glue with a paint scraper. Repeat the procedure to fasten the adjoining rail to the adjacent face of the leg and to glue up the remaining legs with the other rails.

Dowel Joints

Locating and boring dowel holes in the rails

First, mark location points for the dowel holes. Holding one of the rails end-up, set a cutting gauge to one-half the thickness of the stock and scribe a line across the end of the board. With the gauge at a slightly wider setting, etch two marks on the end of the rail that intersect with the first line (right). To avoid splitting the stock, use grooved dowels no more than one-half the thickness of the rails. Fit a drill press or an electric drill with a bit the same diameter as the dowels, then bore a hole at each location point; the depth should be slightly more than one-half the length of the dowels. Use the same technique to bore the dowel holes at the opposite end of the rail and in the other rails.

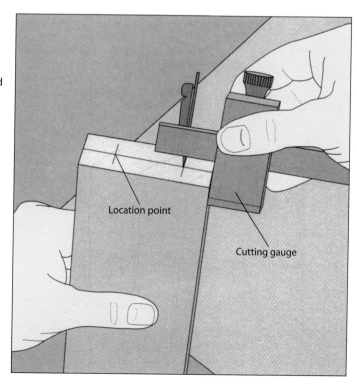

Location point

Cutting gauge

Pinpointing mating dowel holes

Insert dowel centers in the holes. Then align the top of the rail with the top of the leg *(right)*, and swing the rail up so that its outside face is flush with the edge of the leg. Tap the other end of the rail with a wooden mallet. The pointed ends of the dowel centers will punch impressions on the leg, providing starting points for boring the mating dowel holes. Repeat for the other rails and legs.

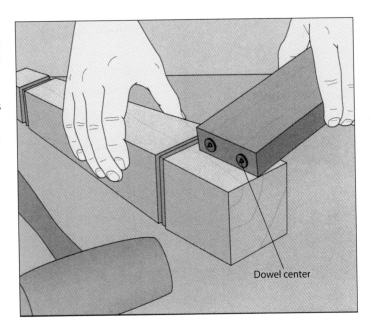

Dowel center

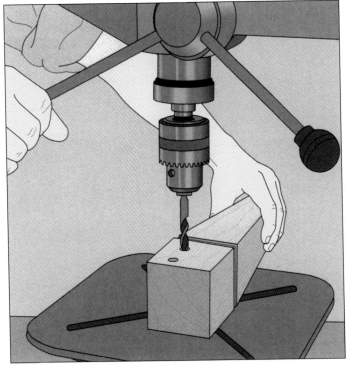

Boring the mating dowel holes and gluing up

Bore the holes in the leg to the same depth as those in the rail *(page 137)*. If you are drilling into a tapered leg on a drill press, be sure to keep the square part of the leg flat on the machine's table. Spread a little glue on the surfaces of the leg and rail that will come into contact with each other, then dab a small amount of adhesive in the bottom of the dowel holes with a pencil tip. Avoid spreading glue directly on the dowels; they absorb moisture quickly and will swell, making them difficult to fit into the holes. Insert the dowels into the legs, then tap them into position with a hammer. Remember not to pound on the dowels, which can cause the leg to split. Fit the rail onto the leg, then close up the joint with the same clamping setup used for the mortise-and-tenon joint *(page 137)*. Glue up the other legs and rails the same way.

Commercial Leg Hardware

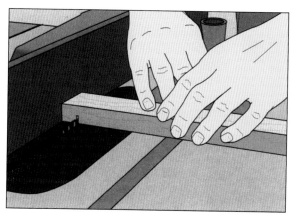

Preparing the rails

Install commercial hardware to attach rails to a leg following the manufacturer's instructions. For the type shown in this section *(page 140)*, test assemble the leg, the rails and the mounting plate, then mark the location of the plate flanges on the rails. To cut the slots for the flanges, align each mark with the blade, then butt the rip fence against the rail. Set the blade height to the length of the flanges, adding ¹⁄₁₆ inch for clearance. Feed the rail into the blade with the miter gauge *(left)*. **(Caution: Blade guard removed for clarity.)** Repeat for the other rail. Slip the flanges into their slots and mark the screw holes on the stock. Bore pilot holes at each point and then screw the mounting plate to the rails.

Preparing the leg

First, cut a notch out of the leg for the mounting plate. Stand the leg up and hold the rail-and-plate assembly on top of it, aligning the ends of the rails with adjacent sides of the leg. Mark a diagonal line across the top of the leg along the mounting plate. Next, align the top of the plate with the top of the leg and mark a line along the bottom edge of the plate across the inside corner of the leg adding ¹⁄₁₆ inch for clearance. To cut the notch, set the leg on a band saw table and tilt the table to align the blade with the diagonal line. Butt a board against the leg and clamp it to the table as a rip fence. Feed the leg into the blade to make the cut, then clamp a stop block in place to help with repeat cuts *(right)*. Complete the notch using a handsaw. Test-assemble the leg and rail-and-plate assembly again and mark the hole on the stock for the hanger bolt provided. Fit your drill press with a brad-point bit and bore a clearance hole for the bolt using a shop-made V-block jig *(inset)*.

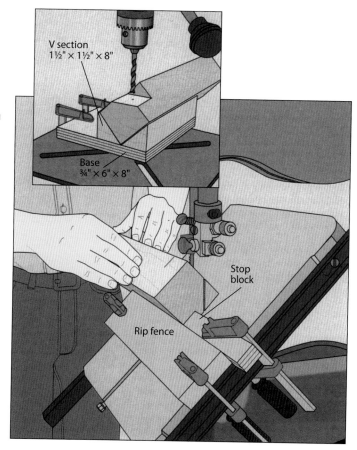

V section
1½" × 1½" × 8"

Base
¾" × 6" × 8"

Stop block

Rip fence

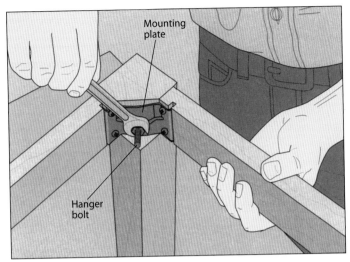

Mounting plate

Hanger bolt

Fastening the leg to the rails

Insert the screw-thread end of the hanger bolt into the clearance hole in the leg. Unlike other fasteners, a hanger bolt has two types of threads: screw threads at one end and bolt threads at the other; it also has no head. Screw nuts onto the bolt-thread end and tighten them against each other with a wrench, forming a temporary head on the bolt. Tighten the bolt with one of the wrenches to drive the screw threads completely into the leg, then unscrew the nuts from the bolt. Slip the rail-and-plate assembly over the bolt and screw a nut on it, making sure that the flanges are in their slots. Keeping the top of the rails flush with the top of the leg, tighten the nut (left).

Shop-Made Leg Hardware

Cutting the corner block

To attach the rails to a leg using shop-made hardware, first make a corner block. Rip a piece of wood narrow enough to drive a hanger bolt through it into the leg. Then make 45° miter cuts at both ends. Next, cut grooves for splines, which will help join the block to the rails. Install a dado head on your table saw with a width and cutting height equal to one-third the thickness of the rails. Screw a board to the miter gauge as an extension, then align the midpoint of one end of the block with the blades. Clamp the block to the extension. Butt a waste piece from the miter cuts against the workpiece to serve as a stop block and clamp it to the extension. Feed the stock into the blades, then turn it over and cut the groove in the other end (right). Test-fit the block against the rails, then mark and cut the grooves. Next, cut a spline for each groove. Plane the splines carefully to make sure that they fit precisely in the matching grooves, remembering to cut them ¹⁄₁₆ short to allow for clearance. For maximum strength, make sure that the grain of the splines runs across their width, rather than along their length.

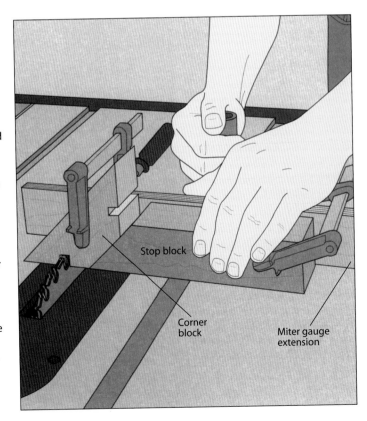

Stop block

Corner block

Miter gauge extension

Boring pilot and clearance holes

Install a brad-point bit on your drill press and mark the center of the long edge of the block for a hanger bolt. Secure the workpiece in a handscrew and clamp it in place as shown, with the center aligned with the bit. Then bore the hole. Next, mark two holes on each side of the clearance hole and drill pilot holes *(right)*, repositioning the block in the handscrew as necessary.

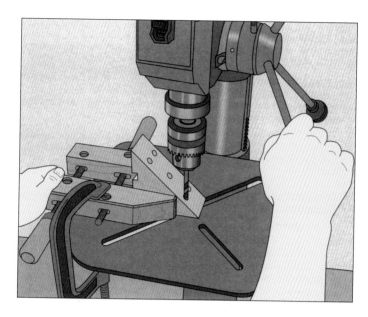

Fastening the leg to the rails

First, fasten the corner block to the rails: Spread some glue in the grooves in the block and the rails, then fit the splines into the grooves in the block. Press the block up against the rails to fit the splines into the rails. Then, keeping the rails snugly against the block, screw the block to the rails *(left)*. Prepare the leg as you would for commercial hardware *(page 139)*, cutting a notch out of the top for the corner block and boring a clearance hole for a hanger bolt. Fasten the leg to the rails with the bolt *(page 140)*, slipping a washer between the nut and the corner block. Tighten the nut *(inset)* until the leg and rails fit snugly together.

Spline

Hanger bolt

Index

Index

Back to Basics

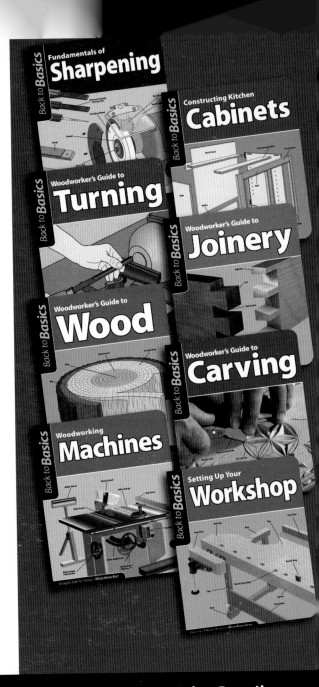